CHINESE CERAMICS

IN THE

AVERY BRUNDAGE COLLECTION

A selection of containers, pillows, figurines, and models from the Neolithic period to modern times.

By René-Yvon Lefebvre d'Argencé

Published by The de Young Museum Society
Distributed by Diablo Press, Berkeley, California

Preface

The de Young Museum Society is proud to be able to publish a handbook of this excellence from the rare collection of Asian Art that Mr. Avery Brundage so generously gave to the City of San Francisco. The Society is indebted to Mr. René-Yvon Lefebvre d'Argencé, Director of the Avery Brundage Foundation, for his continuing interest, effort, and talent in preparing the text and selections of photographic material for *Chinese Ceramics in the Avery Brundage Collection* and to the members of his staff for their efforts in behalf of this publication.

The de Young Museum Society

Chinese Ceramics is the second of a series of volumes presenting a cross-section of the various departments of the Avery Brundage collection of Asian Art. The items shown here do not represent more than 10 percent of the holdings of a department which contains over 1500 objects and is so comprehensive that it could easily furnish all the necessary material for a detailed history of the evolution of Chinese ceramics.

As in the first volume—*Ancient Chinese Bronzes*—our choice was dictated by two criteria: esthetic quality and historical interest. Again, we have felt the difficulties inherent in a selection of this kind. At the time of the international symposium on the arts of Asia which was held in the Brundage Wing in the fall of 1966, some specialists observed that a number of our best or most interesting "pots were not on display but hidden away in storage." Despite the efforts made in this publication to alleviate this shortcoming, we do not feel that we have been entirely successful. Too many fine objects had to be left out because they belong to the category of "historical half-tones"; on the other hand, some significant but not necessarily spectacular landmarks could not be included. Hopefully, the complete catalogue of the collection will in due time satisfy appetites that this series can only stimulate.

I am grateful to the de Young Museum Society for sponsoring this publication, and for their enduring dedication to this project.

Once again, I am indebted to all members of the staff of the Avery Brundage Collection, particularly to Mrs. Margaret Smith, Miss Woan-jen Huang, Miss Yoshiko Kakudo, Mr. Clarence Shangraw, and Mr. Edward Gaston, who by their unreserved collaboration have greatly contributed to the completion of this volume. My thanks also go to Dr. John A. Pope for the kind advice he gave us when we were making our final selection.

Mr. William Abbenseth, our photographer, has repeated his accomplishment of the Bronze catalogue. He is responsible for the photography and for the arrangement of objects within.

Miss Evelyn Bingham has prepared the map and Mr. Steven Warshaw designed the cover.

A number of specimens have been added to the collection in recent years. These we owe to the continuing generosity of Mr. Avery Brundage, whose enthusiasm is achieving wonders even today when the acquisition of important oriental *objets d'art* has become a rather formidable task.

René-Yvon Lefebvre d'Argencé
Director
Avery Brundage Foundation

CONTENTS

Major Kiln Sites in China

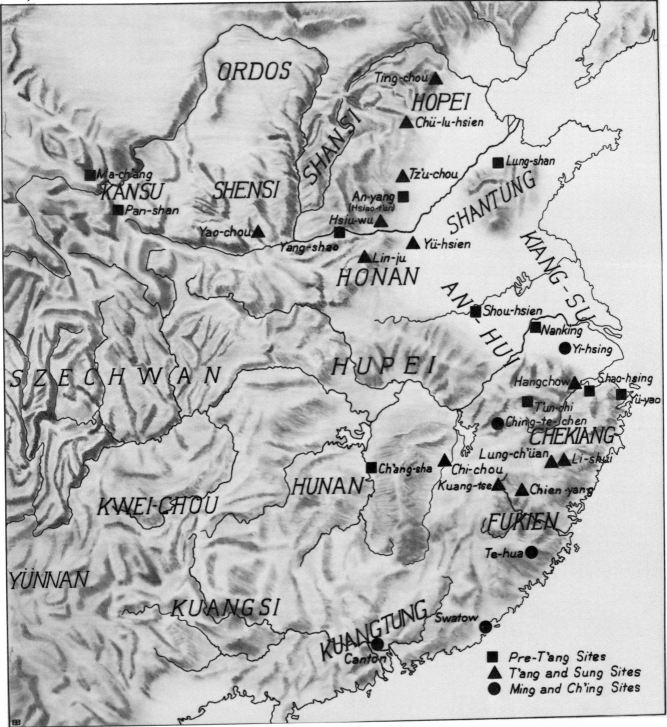

ORDOS

HOPEI

Ting-chou ▲

Chü-lu-hsien ▲

SHANSI

Lung-shan ■

Ma-ch'ang ■

KANSU SHENSI

Tz'u-chou ▲

SHANTUNG

Pan-shan ■

An-yang ■
(Hsiao-t'un)

KIANG-SU

Yao-chou ▲

Hsiu-wu ▲

Yang-shao

Yü-hsien ▲

Lin-ju ▲

HONAN

AN-HUI

Shou-hsien ■

SZECHWAN

HUPEI

Nanking ■

Yi-hsing ●

Hangchow ▲ Shao-hsing

T'un-chi ■ Yü-yao ▲

Ching-te-chen ●

CHEKIANG

Ch'ang-sha ■ Chi-chou ▲ Lung-ch'üan ▲ Li-shui ▲

Kuang-tse ▲ Chien-yang ▲

HUNAN

KWEI-CHOU FUKIEN

Te-hua ●

YÜNNAN

KUANGSI

KUANGTUNG Swatow ●

Canton ●

■ Pre-T'ang Sites
▲ T'ang and Sung Sites
● Ming and Ch'ing Sites

Introduction

It is natural that Chinese ceramics should form the most numerous group of the collection. Paintings, sculptures, bronzes, jades, lacquers and other so-called minor arts illustrate many centuries of artistic activity in China, but only ceramics cover the entire span of approximately forty-five centuries of Chinese history.

Also, ceramics show the greatest diversification. More than any other material, clay was used to serve the needs and satisfy the tastes of all segments of society. Furthermore, at the higher levels of the production, shapes and decorative motifs changed with almost each generation as potters became more sensitive to the influence of other artists and increased their technical knowledge.

A field of this magnitude and diversity was bound to attract art historians. The amount and quality of Chinese, Japanese and Western publications during the past fifty years gave great prominence to the subject of ceramics. But the task is not finished. China's soil has only begun to yield its secrets. Each new excavation can be the source of chronological or typological readjustments. Nevertheless, the current literature on the subject stands out as remarkably comprehensive and reliable.

The Neolithic Period

In China the Neolithic Age lasted for about 3500 years, from *ca.* 5000 to *ca.* 1500 B.C. Like all other similar cultures, it was characterized by the appearance of new tools made of polished stone. This technical revolution was accompanied by other unprecedented factors such as the establishment of a relatively sedentary way of life where agriculture, animal husbandry, and a number of crafts, including pottery-making, occupied an important place.

The earliest pieces of Chinese pottery discovered so far have been dated to about 3000 B.C. Neolithic pottery sites are well distributed over the country, especially along its three main rivers, the Huangho in the north, the Yangtzekiang in the center and the Sikiang in the south. The highest density of sites and also the earliest specimens were found in the Huangho basin, that "cradle of Chinese civilization."

Neolithic pottery is conveniently divided into three main categories according to its color—red, black and gray. Each category is also known by the name of a type-site: Yang-shao in western Honan for Red Pottery, Lung-shan in Shantung for Black Pottery and Hsiao-t'un near An-yang in northern Honan for Gray Pottery (Pl. 1-B). The geographical distribution of these categories and their respective chronologies are still under study. There was apparently considerable overlapping between the various types in the central provinces, especially in Honan and Shansi. Yet, archaeologists have been able to distinguish between a Yang-shao culture prevailing in the western highlands and a Lung-shan culture prevailing in the eastern and southeastern lowlands. The Hsiao-t'un culture is thought to have flourished at the crossroads of the other two or to have emerged from their fusion. In any event, it exerted its influence far and wide throughout the land and set the foundation for historical China (Pls. IV, V-A, B).

The Shang and Chou Dynasties

This period of approximately a millennium and a half corresponds to the Chinese Bronze Age. It was marked by the appearance of many new pottery shapes, frequently related to those of bronze vessels (Pls. IV, V-B) and by some startling technical improvements.

As early as Shang times, metropolitan potters knew how to select, levigate and fire clay to make vessels of almost pure white quality and of stoneware hardness (Pl. VI). Apparently, they also knew how to protect the outer surface of some of their wares with a vitreous substance (see Pl. V-C for a somewhat later example). Some specialists regard this coating as the first manifestation of ceramic glazes.

Functional as they may have been initially, beater's marks were astutely exploited for decorative purposes. Late Shang and Chou potters conceived a wide range of geometric arrangements obtained not only by beating but also stamping, incising, and rouletting. Some motifs resemble those of Bronze art (Pls. V through VIII), but others were restricted to ceramic products.

Early in the Chou period, glazing became common, at least in the Wu-Yüeh region (Pls. V-C, VIII); toward the end of the same period, painting with rich mineral pigments was revived after many centuries of interruption (Pl. IX-B).

The earliest clay figurines in the round can be traced back to the Neolithic period, but specimens remained rare and coarse until late in the Warring States period when such groups as the Hui-hsien and Fen-shui-ling sets foreshadow the ming-ch'i (grave goods) of later periods.

The Han Dynasty

The introduction of lead and feldspathic glazes colored with a variety of metallic oxides, such as those derived from copper and iron, was a spectacular achievement, during this first imperial dynasty (Pls. IX through XI). In addition to technical achievements, this period is noted for mortuary pottery and funerary sculpture in clay where human and animal figurines mingled with buildings and models of household furniture of all kinds as they did in real life (Pls. XI through XIII). It is interesting to note that in China, man and his environment, including natural settings and embryonic landscapes (Pls. X-A, B) were first represented in noticeable quantities as a result of new funerary rites. Beyond an obvious refinement of the traditional concepts of ancestor worship, this "humanization" of Chinese art reflected the increasing influence of the two great Chinese philosophies, Confucianism and Taoism.

The Six Dynasties

Recent excavations make it possible to describe the ceramic art of this troubled period in more than general terms. The discovered grave goods show that the Han spirit and techniques lingered on (Pl. XI-C). Originally, Buddhism, the great revolutionary movement of the time, did not affect these objects directly because this religion was more concerned with the living than with the dead. By the sixth century, however, the cosmopolitanism and urbanization that are associated with Buddhism resulted in a change of the choice of subjects (Pl. VI). Concurrently, Buddhist styles as we know them in sculpture and painting influenced figurine makers. In this domain, the most conspicuous contributions of the period are more accurate proportions for heads and bodies, flowing, elegant attitudes and a more detailed, more nervous rendering of the folds of garments.

Although figurine makers continued to rely heavily on unfired pigments, for surface decorations, progress was also made in the preparation and application of a small group of monochrome glazes used to protect and adorn utilitarian wares. Especially noteworthy are the proto-celadons of the region of Wu and Yüeh, produced as early as the 3rd century A.D. (Pls. XIV and XV).

The Sui and T'ang Dynasties

These imperial dynasties ruled for three centuries, at a time of internal euphory and increased international intercourse. Sophisticated household and ornamental objects, as well as grave goods of higher technical quality, were in great demand. Craftsmen, including potters, produced new ideas and techniques to satisfy their fastidious clients.

Monochromic and dichromic ware frequently show simple, sturdy forms with tense, bulging contours and a wide variety of even glazes ranging from white to black with a large proportion of light yellows and brilliant greens (Pls. XVII through XX). One group of highly fired, thin-bodied vessels with an almost pure white glaze is of special interest because it represents the earliest example of true porcelain (Pl. XX).

Often inspired by metallic prototypes of Persian origin, polychromes can have more angular and agitated contours. By blending rich and warm glazes, potters created opulent color schemes. This series reflects the spirit of a period which developed a taste for precious materials and brilliant decorative effects Pl. XXVI). The preceding period had already shown a predilection for exotic and courtly subjects; this trend now reached its full maturity (Pls. XXI through XXV). Furthermore, direct borrowings from the Buddhist pantheon are no longer exceptional (Pl. XXI-A). Painted figurines, continued to be made but quite naturally, sculptors also availed themselves of the progress made in the coloring of glazes. This decorative device often added an abstract touch to forms which are otherwise remarkably realistic (Pl. XXV-C).

The Liao Dynasty

This period offers an interesting example of a partial fossilization of styles and techniques through foreign immixture. For about 200 years the Khitan Mongols occupied much of north China. Their pottery retained the essential characteristics of the T'ang period, although there was a considerable rarefaction in the variety of shapes, glazes, and decorative motifs (Pl. XXVII). On the other hand, Liao potters created indigenous and highly original objects (Pl. XXVIII).

The Five Dynasties and the Sung Dynasty

In the 10th century the efforts of generations of Yüeh potters to improve their glazes were fully rewarded. Kilns in the region of Hang-chou and Shao-hsing, in the heart of the autonomous Wu-Yüeh kingdom, produced a superior celadon, known as Pi-ssu (Pl. XXIX). At first, this ware was made for the local court, but its reputation soon spread far and wide. When the Sung re-established imperial rule, this celadon received official recognition and served as a model for many northern productions. Yüeh celadons were also exported to Korea where they probably played an important part in the initial phase of the development of the famed Koryo celadons.

During the Northern Sung period, governmental recognition and sponsorship largely contributed to cause a "ceramic explosion." Numerous new kilns were built and old ones revived, especially in the metropolitan area (Honan and neighboring provinces). Many kilns specialized in the manufacture of specific types and glazes—celadons at Ju-chou and Yao-chou (Pls. XXX and XXXI), white, thin-bodied wares at Ting-chou (Pls. XXXII through XXXIV), and heavily potted, thick glazed, blue-tinted vessels at Chün-chou, T'ang-ying hsien, and Hsiu-wu (Pls. XXXV and XXXVI).

These phenomena, explosion and specialization, were accompanied by a third one of equal significance: the bifurcation of the ceramic industry into so-called official and folk wares. The former, the more sophisticated and more expensive, reflected an aristocratic and slightly effeminate taste for simple, dainty shapes and subtle monochrome glazes. The latter, primarily destined to the less fortunate or to a less noble use, show a predilection for vigorous designs in contrasted and frequently brilliant colors (Pls. XXVII through XL).

During the Southern Sung period, several kilns such as those of the regions of Hang-chou, Ching-te-chen, and Lung-ch'üan retained northern official traditions (Pls. XLI through XLV.) Others, while maintaining standards of quality generally associated with high levels of ceramic production, began to adopt some "rustic" attitudes such as polychromism and underglaze-painted decoration. (Pls. XLVI and XLVII). This syncretic approach, timid as it was initially, coincided with one of the most dramatic moments in the history of Chinese ceramics. On the one hand it formed a tangible link with pre-Sung achievements, on the other hand it set the pattern for the main trend in future developments.

The Yüan and Ming Dynasties

In the fourteenth century Ching-te-chen became the ceramic metropolis of China. Many other kilns remained active, and a few of them, such as Lung-ch'üan, continued to operate on a large scale for the national and international markets (Pl. XLVIII-C); but none of them could compete with Ching-te-chen, which benefited from extraordinary facilities in the supply of combustibles and raw materials including rich kaolin deposits in the vicinity. Even though direct governmental intervention was negligible during the Mongol rule, potters of this privileged region managed to refine the production of several monochrome series and more particularly of white and light blue glazes, best represented by the celebrated Shu-fu and Ch'ing-pai wares (Pl. XLVIII A and B). Simultaneously, they initiated new techniques to solve the arduous problem of combining rich, colorful painted motifs with porcelain bodies and highly vitrified, transparent glazes. Today, most specialists agree that the first "underglaze red" and "blue and white" porcelains were made early in the fourteenth century (Pl. XLIX), long before the return of Chinese rule and the establishment of government-controlled kilns at Ching-te-chen.

Starting from the first quarter of the fifteenth century, court supervision became such a determining factor that the changing tastes of the consecutive monarchs and their advisors inspired a succession of styles which can be delineated over short periods of time, sometimes even from one decade to another.

Throughout the Ming dynasty blue-and-white porcelains formed the bulk of the production. The reigns of Hsüan Te (Pls. L and LI), Ch'eng Hua, Cheng Te (Pl. LIII-A), Chia Ching (Pl. LIII-B and LIV), and Wan Li (Pl. LV), are particularly noted for the quality of their wares and the originality of their styles.

Some of the finest monochromes were made during the reigns of Yung Lo, Hsüan Te, and Chia Ching (Pl. LVI). In the seventeenth century, independent kilns at Te-hua in Fukien province developed a highly original style which can be regarded as the only major sculptural trend of the period (Pl. LVII).

Beginning with the reign of Ch'eng Hua, there was a renewed interest in polychrome effects based on enameling and medium-temperature glazes. The collection contains an assortment of wares decorated in two, three and five colors (Pls. LVIII through LXIII). The last category, the most elaborate, sometimes exceedingly so, reached its highest development during the Hung Chih and Wan Li periods. (Pl. LXII). Other fine examples are also a provincial group of export porcelains known as Swatow wares (Pl. LXIII).

The Ch'ing Dynasty

The last imperial dynasty of foreign origin, is noted for three main styles corresponding to the reigns of K'ang Hsi, Yung Cheng and Ch'ien Lung. Each of these styles came to maturity at the imperial factory of Ching-te-chen under the directorships of Ts'ang Ying-hsüan for the K'ang Hsi period, Nien Hsi-yao for the Yung Cheng period and T'ang Ying for the earlier part of the Ch'ien Lung period.

K'ang Hsi potters perfected existing series while gradually developing bolder ornamental schemes largely inspired by contemporary landscape and genre paintings. They also introduced a new range of monochrome colors (Pls. LXIV and LXV) and of enamel-painted wares known as the Famille Noire and Famille Verte types (Pls. LXVI through LXIX).

The monochrome, blue-and-white, and underglaze groups of the Yung Cheng and Ch'ien Lung periods often show an archaistic taste (Pls. LXX, LXXI and LXXII). Yet, these reigns have remained unsurpassed in the ingenuousness and audacity they displayed in their use of opaque enamels of the Famille Rose type (Pls. LXXIII, LXXIV and LXXV).

The Ch'ing period is also known for its numerous adaptations of Western techniques and decorative motifs.

PLATE I

A. LI-TRIPOD, Red Pottery

Neolithic period
(3rd millenium B.C.)
H: 4" W: 5¼"   B60P430
Published: W. Hochstadter, *"Pottery and Stonewares of Shang, Chou and Han."*
BMFEA 1952, No. 24, Pl. I, fig. 1
R.-Y Lefebvre d'Argencé, *"Early Chinese Ceramics in the Avery Brundage Collection,"*
Apollo, Aug. 1966, p. 85, fig. 2

B. LI-TRIPOD, Gray Pottery

Late Neolithic period
(*ca.* 2000 B.C.)
H: 6" W: 5¼"   B60P2074
Published: d'Argencé *op. cit.,* p. 84, fig. 1

These vessels are variants of the most typical shape of Chinese pottery in its formative phase. Unknown outside the Chinese world, this shape seems to have originated in the northern provinces of Shansi and Honan.

Basically, the Li-tripod is an assemblage of three hollow, voluminous legs with swelling contours and smooth articulations. Some scholars suggested that this intriguing silhouette resulted from the joining of three jars with pointed bottoms. Others, with a symbolic turn of mind, believe that the mammary allusion was too conspicuous to be accidental. All concur that the tripod was remarkably well designed for rapid and thorough cooking.

Made from a coarse paste of common clay tempered with sand, such vessels were modeled by hand, usually by the coiling method. They were baked at low temperature and remained largely porous.

(A) This archetype is characterized by the absence of additional features or surface embellishments. The bulging legs recede evenly toward a slightly triangular neck. The short, vertical mouth rim seems to indicate that another container was meant to fit over this vessel, in which case it served as the lower part of a Hsien steamer (See *Bronze Handbook,* Pl. XXVII-A.)

(B) This more elaborate version is well represented by numerous discoveries made in northern sites of both the Lung-shan and Yang-shao cultures. Its main features are a flat handle, a tall, plain neck, and a regular "corduroy" pattern all around the legs. This decorative ribbing is the result of a special technique in which the potter hardened his paste and reduced its thickness by beating the surface of the vessel with a wooden spatula covered with cord, mat, or similar materials. Thus, this type of decoration is also known as "beater's marks."

B.

A.

PLATE II

A. URN, Painted Pottery

Late Neolithic, Yang-shao culture,
Pan-shan style (2500–2000 B.C.)
H: 9½″ W: 8½″   B60P1836

B. LONG-NECKED VASE, Painted Pottery

Late Neolithic, Yang-shao culture
Pan-shan style (2500–2000 B.C.)
H: 9½″ W: 9½″   B60P2272
Published: d'Argencé *op. cit.*, p. 86, fig. 3

C. JAR, Painted Pottery

Late Neolithic, Yang-shao culture,
From Chu-chia chai, Huang-chung hsien,
Chinghai province. (*ca.* 2000 B.C.)
H: 5¾″ D: 6½″   B66P40

The northwestern provinces of Kansu and Chinghai have yielded some of the most advanced types of Neolithic ceramics.

(A) The hilly cemetery of Pan-shan in central Kansu is perhaps best known for this kind of urns with large globular bodies, low necks, flaring mouths, flat bases, and two small loop handles placed near the greatest diameter.

When the curved line was a favorite motif among potters of the Yang-shao culture, Pan-shan urns were noted for the sweeping rhythm of bold variegated spirals not to be found elsewhere in China. The design stops short of the base and is bordered by a straight line above a wavy band.

(B) This is basically the same shape, but its size and elongated neck indicate that it served as a pourer rather than a container. The mouth rim is equipped with two crenellated lugs to give a better grip.

As in the globular urn, areas in the painted design show a saw-tooth pattern, also known as the "death pattern" because it was apparently restricted to vessels made to be buried with the dead.

(C) This small jar was found in Chinghai province just across the border from Ma-ch'ang (Pl. III). It is one of the very few items which have entered the collection with an official certificate of excavation. The jars of that region have a squattish appearance, and designs occupy a wider area on the bellies. On the other hand, concentric circles inscribed with a criss-cross pattern are well attested in the Ma-ch'ang complex. (Pl. III).

A.

B.

C.

PLATE III

URN, Painted Pottery

Late Neolithic, Yang-shao culture
Ma-ch'ang style (2000–1500 B.C.)
H: 14″ D: 12″   B60P1110
Published: d'Argencé, *op. cit.*, p. 85, Pl. I

The Neolithic "painted pottery" of northern China is related in style to
several groups found in central and western Asia. Local clay throwers, working with a
turntable, if not a wheel, favored a special kind of red clay which could be potted
very thin. They took pains to give a superior finish to their ware, patiently burnished
surfaces and decorated the upper part of the vessel in orange, red, brown or black.
The mineral pigments are so resistant that they still frequently retain most of their
original brilliance.

There is a wide range of shapes and dimensions but the basic forms are large urns,
bottle-shaped vessels, basins and bowls. Painted designs are usually geometric but
sometimes anthropomorphic and zoomorphic. Possibly, they were conceived to embody
some symbolic meanings which are now almost completely lost.

Ma-ch'ang, in Kansu, was both a cemetery and a dwelling site. Urns found there
frequently have a narrow base and a projecting mouth rim. The use of colors is
less lavish than at Pan-shan. (Pl. II). The main motif illustrated here is thought to be
anthropomorphic. It may have served as a model for the more explicit versions of
early historic times (Pl. VI).

PLATE IV

A. KU, Gray Pottery

Late Shang period, An-yang style
(1300–1028 B.C.)
H: 6¼″ W: 4⅛″   B60P1831
Published: d'Argencé *op. cit.*, p. 87, fig. 6

B. CHÜEH-TRIPOD, Gray Pottery

Late Shang period, An-yang style,
(1300–1028 B.C.)
H: 4¾″ W: 4¼″   B60P1834

The Shang dynasty marks the beginnings of the Chinese Bronze Age. The casting of
bronze vessels necessitated a number of technical operations such as the making
of crucibles, models and molds which owed a great deal to well-established ceramic
traditions. In this sense, it can be said that Shang bronze casters were the direct heirs of
the Neolithic potters. Conversely, it must be recognized that the predominant role
played by bronze in the higher levels of artistic productions during the Shang
and Western Chou periods somewhat hampered the stylistic evolution of pottery as an
independent art.

Traditional shapes of the gray pottery of the Hsiao-t'un type are so similar to
Neolithic shapes that there is no practical way to tell the difference. New forms, like
those illustrated here, are imitations of bronze models (See *Bronze Handbook,*
Pls. VIII, X). They probably served as cheap substitutes, to be buried with the dead.

Both vessels are made from a coarse paste with thick walls and hardly any decoration,
Despite these technical defects they convey a feeling of well-balanced and simple
sturdiness which makes them attractive to the modern eye.

This simplicity is not as artless as it appears to be at first glance. In both cases the
potter was able to produce vessels which are structurally easily distinguishable
from their bronze counterparts by their proportions, the absence of uprights and tail in
the Chüeh (*B*), and the disposition and size of the flanges in the Ku (*A*).

A.

B.

PLATE V

A. JAR, Gray Pottery

Late Shang period
(1300–1028 B.C.)
From An-yang (Honan)
H: 4¾″ W: 5½″   B60P431
Published: Hochstadter, *op. cit.*, Pl. 8, No. 29
d'Argencé, *op. cit.*, p. 87, fig. 7

B. KUEI-BOWL, Gray Pottery

Late Shang period
(1300–1028 B.C.)
From An-yang (Honan)
H: 4½″ D: 6¼″   P60P433
Published: Hochstadter, *op. cit.*, Pl. 4, No. 16
d'Argencé, *op. cit.*, p. 87, fig. 8

C. BOWL, Stoneware, Olive-Green Glaze

Late Western Chou
(*ca.* 800 B.C.)
Probably from Anhwei province
H: 2″ D: 4″   B60P223
Published: Hochstadter, *op. cit.*, Pl. 27, No. 107
d'Argencé, *op. cit.*, p. 89, fig. 11

(*A*) (*B*) These specimens of gray pottery show several advanced features compared with the pottery of the previous plate. They were made at or near An-yang, the last capital of the Shang state.

Pastes are denser as a result of more careful levigation and walls are consequently less porous. Because of the use of a fairly sophisticated wheel, shapes are better balanced although perhaps more commonplace. Surfaces are burnished and decorated with incised geometric designs: chevrons for the jar, (*A*), crosshatching for the stem cup (*B*). Both vessels are also adorned with concentric grooves on necks and feet. The molded projections on the neckband of the stem cup imitate the flanges and bosses of contemporary bronzes. (See *Bronze Handbook* Pls. III, IV).

(*C*) Only very few specimens of this material have been found for the Shang dynasty and none for the early Western Chou period. However, Late Western Chou vessels of the type illustrated here have been excavated repeatedly in the southern part of Anhwei province and Chinese archaeologists believe they help fill the gap between Shang and post-Western Chou productions. The ornamental scheme on the neck zone is not unlike that of the Shang Kuei (*B*), although it is rendered in "mat impression" instead of being incised. The small three-stranded loop handles terminate in molded spirals. The glaze is thick, uneven, and seems to have flaked away in parts.

A.

B.

C.

PLATE VI

COVERED JAR, White Pottery

Late Shang period
(1300–1028 B.C.)
From An-yang (Honan)
H: 8" D: 8⅝"   B60P538
Published: S. Umehara, *Kanan Anyō Ibutsu no Kenkyū,* Kyoto, 1941, Pls. VIII, X
Sekai Kōkogaku Taikei, Tokyo 1958, No. 6, fig. 360
Cheng Te-k'un, *Shang China,* Pl. XXXI-B
d'Argencé, *op. cit.,* p. 89, fig. 9

This is one of the most sophisticated and rarest vessels of Shang pottery. Found broken in pieces, it was reconstructed with infinite care by the eminent Japanese archaeologist Sueji Umehara. (The darker or plain areas are patches).

To produce such wares, Shang potters used a clay carefully levigated and baked it to stoneware hardness at approximately 1000°C. Shapes and decor suggest contemporary sacrificial bronze vessels. These containers were too delicate to be used for daily life and probably served ceremonial or funerary purposes. However, far from being an imitation of bronze models, this vessel, one of five or six in existence, reflects a skillful blending of old ceramic and more recent metallic traditions.

This vessel somewhat resembles specimens of the p'ou or chih groups of bronze vessels (see *Bronze Handbook* Pls. XIV-A, XVII) but its proportions do not belong to either category, nor do the distribution of its curved decorative motifs or the nature of its main ornamental scheme. The latter, a highly dissolved, geometricized and partly anthropomorphic pattern in high relief against a background of meanders, is not unknown in Shang bronze art where it always appears in connection with a human mask or eye motifs, such as the one shown here on the neck zone. But the present silhouettes seem to stand in between some Neolithic representations (Pl. III) and bronze specimens.

PLATE VII

A. HU-SHAPED TRIPOD, Gray Pottery

Warring States period, Chin-ts'un style
(5th to 3rd Century B.C.)
H: 12½″ W: 7½″   B60P1825
Published: Hochstadter, *op. cit.,* Pl. 19, No. 74

B. TING TRIPOD, Gray Pottery

Warring States period
(*ca.* 4th Century B.C.)
H: 13″ W: 12½″   B60P1824
Published: Hochstadter, *op. cit.,* Pl. 18, No. 72

Throughout the Eastern Chou period, potters continued working along the lines established during the Shang and Western Chou dynasties. One of their main tasks was to satisfy an increasing demand for funerary wares, many of which tended to become less simplified although frequently clumsier copies of bronze models.

(A) There is no single metallic prototype for such tripods, rather they seem to result from the blending of several type forms. The body is that of a Hu but the legs belong to other categories. With the exception of four parallel horizontal grooves the body is plain. The animals (dogs?) on the shoulder have their heads turned completely backward in an unusual position, and their arched bodies form loop handles. Similar or identical vessels have been unearthed from Chin-ts'un tombs near Lo-yang in Honan.

(B) This almost exact copy of a bronze Ting has also been reported as a Lo-yang find, but it looks so strikingly like certain bronze specimens recently discovered at Chia-ko-chuang near T'ang-shan in Hopei that it is probably of northern origin. Particularly revealing are the excessive development of the handles and legs, the bold treatment of the unicorn "t'ao-t'ieh" masks above the legs, and the way the bodies of the felines on the lid are done in low relief in contrast to their curved necks and anxious heads, which project out above the surface and give them a giraffe-like appearance. The only features the potter has not tried to recapture are the sweeping curvatures of the bronze handles and the usual vermiculous motifs of the neck band. The latter have been replaced here by a highly imaginative if wholly geometric scheme which to our knowledge is without parallel in the art of the Bronze Age.

A.

B.

PLATE VIII

A. YI-TRIPOD, Glazed Stoneware

Warring States period
(5th to 3rd Century B.C.)
Yüeh type
H: 6″ W: 4″   B60P225
Published: Hochstadter, *op. cit.*, Pl. 27, No. 106
d'Argencé, *op. cit.*, p. 90, fig. 114

B. BELL, Glazed Stoneware

Warring States period
(5th to 3rd Century B.C.)
Yüeh type
H: 6″ W: 4″   B60P196
Published: d'Argencé, *op. cit.*, p. 90, fig. 13

Eastern Chou craftsmen strove to perfect the method of glazing ceramic wares.
Already in Warring States time several kilns of the Wu-Yüeh area succeeded in putting
out a stoneware with an even, translucent and resistant coating. This was a decisive
improvement and an important step on the road toward the production of full-fledged
porcelain. Such glazed wares were probably first produced for the market of grave
goods (Ming-ch'i) but during the Han dynasty, when they continued to be made in
great quantity, they took mostly the form of large jars for daily use or for storage.

During the Warring States period, the taste in funerary furniture was dictated by
that of the bronze casters as seen in these examples. (Compare, for instance,
Bronze Handbook. Pl. XLVI-C). We find here the same approach and the same
simplification discussed in connection with the northern pieces illustrated on the
preceding plate. Structures and ornaments are different in the two groups because these
two objects take after a different metallic tradition, such as that illustrated by the
Shou-hsien finds in Anhwei. Here potters have replaced open-work features by simple
break contours and the usual grumous surfaces by a maze of stamped spirals for the
Yi and by a casual arrangement of stamped circles for the bell.

A.   *B.*

PLATE IX

A. HU-VASE, Glazed Stoneware

Western Han dynasty
(2nd to 1st Century B.C.)
Yüeh type
H: 18" D: 14¾"   B60P81+
Published: d'Argencé, *op. cit.*, p. 88, Pl. II

B. HU-VASE, Painted Pottery

Late Warring States—Western Han dynasty
(3rd to 1st Century B.C.)
H: 23" D: 16"   B60P2391
Published: d'Argencé, *op. cit.*, p. 91, fig. 17

C. HU-VASE, Pottery With Iridescent Glaze

Han dynasty
(206 B.C.–221 A.D.)
H: 22" D: 12½"   B60P1115

The Hu vases of the late Warring States and Han periods are very diversified depending on regional or technical characteristics but they seldom can conceal their metallic lineage. This is best shown by the presence of the applied T'ao-t'ieh masks which decorate the shoulders of our examples.

(A) With its gray porcelaneous body fired to stoneware hardness, its shoulders covered with a thin and uneven layer of dark olive-green feldspathic glaze, its reddish surface where the paste has been directly exposed to kiln fire and its flat base, this vessel typifies the early phase of a celebrated Chekiang ware which shows some affinities with the pottery discussed in Plate VIII and is consequently regarded by several specialists as the second step toward the making of the reputed Yüeh celadons. The shoulder bears two zones of incised "birdicized clouds," a typical Han motif. The animal masks, small, in low-relief and placed very high on the shoulder are connected with large bow-shaped handles with an incised pattern of herring bones. The small, rope-like rings which "hang" from these handles are fossilized vestiges of bronze prototypes.

(B) Starting from the later part of the Warring States period, grave goods makers began to paint motifs on their products inspired by models found in goldsmithing or lacquer work. These intertwining cloud scrolls with faintly suggested animal shapes are characteristic of the kind. They are painted in red, white and indigo with red outlines.

(C) This red pottery Hu with a green iridescent glaze exemplifies a category which was made in almost industrial quantity by northern potters. The lid with its molded mountains and waves is the most ornate part of the vessel. Such Hu were possibly destined to form parts of sets where hill jars occupied a central place (Pl. X).

B.

C.   A.

PLATE X

A. HILL JAR, Pottery With Iridescent Glaze

Han dynasty
(206 B.C.–221 A.D.)
H: 10″ D: 8″   B60P236
Published: d'Argencé, *op. cit.*, p. 91, fig. 18

B. PO-SHAN-LU, Incense Burner, Pottery

Han dynasty
(206 B.C.–221 A.D.)
H: 9″ D: 7¼″   B60P203

C. DRAGON, Painted Pottery

Eastern Han or Early Six dynasties
(3rd to 4th Century A.D.)
H: 7¾″ L: 9½″   B60P324
Published: d'Argencé *op. cit.*, p. 92, fig. 21

During the first centuries of this era, animal life became a major source of inspiration for grave goods makers. Together with domestic animals (see next plate), wild or fabulous beasts were often sculptured either as individual figurines or as decorative motifs in high relief. The latter are often shown as the main characters of hunting scenes taking place in natural settings, which rank among the earliest representations of landscapes in Chinese art.

(A) This particular shape was perhaps derived from the blending of two bronze forms such as the Lien and the Po-shan-lu (see *Bronze Handbook* Pls. LIII, LV-B). Characteristic of the entire group are the cylindrical body, the animal feet, and the molded decoration on the cover and the cylinder. The cover exhibits the usual pattern of mountains and waves suggestive of Mount P'eng Lai, the Great Central Mountain of Taoist paradise, rising in the middle of the Gray Jade Ocean. The central band shows a mythical hunting scene which looks like a simplified version of the theme illustrated on our gilt bronze Lien B60B951 (see *Bronze Handbook* Pl. LIII-B). The feet are in the form of three squatting bears.

(B) This object is distinguished from the numerous series of Han incense burners by the complexity of the ornamental scheme of its cover, and also by the contrast it makes with the bare lower part. Here the hunting scene unrolls from right to left and in two main horizontal registers. Altogether it contains twenty-five participants of which seventeen are animals (including a dragon, a lizard and a bear) and eight hunters. The men use a variety of weapons and hounds. There is, however, no real shooting or killing, with the exception of a particularly violent episode which shows a tiger devouring a man.

A.

B.

C.

PLATE XI

A. DOG, Brown-Glazed Pottery

Han dynasty (206 B.C.–221 A.D.)
Ch'ang-sha type
H: 14¾" L: 13½"   B60P83+
Published: d'Argencé, *op. cit.,* p. 92, fig. 19

B. DOG, Green-Glazed Pottery

Han dynasty (206 B.C.–221 A.D.)
Ch'ang-sha type
H: 14" L: 15"   B60P306
Published: d'Argencé, *op. cit.,* p. 92, fig. 20

C. LANCER, Painted Pottery

Late Eastern Han or Western Chin period
(3rd Century A.D.)
H: 15½" W: 9"   B60P302

As the demand for grave goods swept all over China, clay throwers had to become sculptors as well. Their figurines show marked regional characteristics such as those discussed in connection with vessels, but as a rule they reflect consistently the same notional approach, whose roots can easily be traced back to Shang times. In keeping with their predecessors, Han figurine makers could be surprisingly realistic when they wanted, but as a rule, they did not aim at verisimilitude. They were more interested in capturing lively expressions and postures, and were particularly fascinated by the outstanding characteristic features of their subjects. Hence the caricatural appearance of many of their products, the enormous heads with exaggerated facial features, and the lumpy bodies that are treated rather cursorily and seem to serve almost exclusively as channels for an energy which is kept latent until it reaches explosive heads. At the same time, Han or Early Six Dynasties grave goods makers served primarily farmers or warriors and, therefore, most of their figurines are done in a charming bucolic, almost naive vein.

(*A*) and (*B*) Although these watch-dogs are shown in different positions and colored differently, the nature of the clay and glazes and the similarity of the facial features point to a common origin. They represent a series which is well attested in Ch'ang-sha (Hunan province).

A.

C.

B.

PLATE XII

A. FIGURINES, Painted Pottery

Eastern Han or Early Six dynasties
(2nd to 4th Century A.D.)
H: 4″   B60P1252

B. FARMYARD, Green-Glazed Pottery

Han dynasty
(206 B.C.–221 A.D.)
H: 4″ L: 8¾″   B60P229

C. FARMHOUSE, Pottery

Eastern Han dynasty
(1st to 3rd Century A.D.)
Ch'ang-sha type
H: 8″ W: 8½″   B60P1215
Published: d'Argencé, *op. cit.,* p. 91, fig. 16

One of the major contributions of Han potters is their emphasis on the various manifestations of human life and on man's environment. This emphasis was precipitated by new religious practices and the necessity of manufacturing large quantities of cheap substitutes of household objects (ming-ch'i) which could be buried with the dead to make them feel at home in their after-life.

Han potters reproduced nearly all aspects of the society they lived in. They showed both sexes, all ages from infancy to confirmed venerability, and various racial types.

Human figurines are found in a variety of situations—idle, conversing, dancing, playing music or games, or engaged in other typical activities (Pl. XI). When bodies are treated summarily, heads are often disproportionally large. The masks of large figurines reflect such moods as fear, ferocity, contentment, surprise, or polite attention. In narrative group scenes, such as the ones illustrated here, emphasis is placed on attitudes—there is little attempt to depict individual components in detail.

(A) This set of four statuettes was part of the decoration of a funerary jar on whose shoulder they were standing or climbing. One of them is carrying a bag of cereals.

(B) Here a farmer is pounding grain while being watched by a dog and two domestic fowls. Next to him is a millstone.

(C) Architectural models of this kind are usually faithful copies of wooden or brick structures.

A.

B.

C.

PLATE XIII

A. SILO, Pottery

Western Han dynasty
(2nd to 1st Century B.C.)
Ch'ang-sha type
H: 7" D: 9"   B60P221

B. CLUSTER OF JARS, Pottery

Western Han dynasty
(2nd to 1st Century B.C.)
Ch'ang-sha type
H: 3" W: 8"   B60P206

C. LONG-NECKED JAR, Stoneware

Western Han dynasty
(2nd to 1st Century B.C.)
Kuangtung type
H: 9" D: 8"   B60P437

(A) and (B) Early during the Han dynasty, Southern potters, particularly those of Hunan and Kuangtung provinces, produced a great number of ming-ch'i (grave goods), which are more crisply potted and decorated than most Northern wares (see also Pl. XII-C).

They favored a buff paste, sparsely coated with a thin, flaky feldspathic glaze. The geometric patterns have by now lost all symbolic significance and are incised in very sharp lines. They contrast vividly with the rather amorphous moldings of standard Northern wares.

(C) This unusual vessel is another example of the taste prevailing among Southern potters of the Western Han period. It is not a funerary item, but a sturdy object made for every-day use. It was baked to stoneware hardness, and its ash glaze surface has been burnished; its broad, flat base gives it remarkable stability. The decor consists of thirteen narrow bands of parallel slanting lines, crosshatchings, tooth motifs, and wave patterns. These designs are partly incised, partly combed, and partly rouletted. The casual way in which they were executed contrasts with the complexity of the techniques involved.

A.

B.

C.

PLATE XIV

A. LION-SHAPED CONTAINER, Glazed Stoneware

> Western Chin dynasty
> (265–316 A.D.)
> Yüeh type
> H: 3¼" L: 4¾"   B60P1482

B. INK STAND, Glazed Stoneware

> Western Chin dynasty
> (265–316 A.D.)
> Yüeh type
> H: 3¼" D: 5"   B60P231
> Published: d'Argencé, *op. cit.,* p. 93, Pl. IV

C. JAR, Glazed Stoneware

> Wu or Western Chin dynasty
> (3rd to 4th Century A.D.)
> Yüeh type
> H: 4⅞" D: 5½"   B60P1585

D. COVERED BOWL, Glazed Stoneware

> Six dynasties
> (4th–5th Century A.D.)
> Yüeh type
> H: 3" D: 4"   B60P145
> Published: d'Argencé, *op. cit.,* p. 94, fig. 24

Yüeh potters of the region of present-day Nanking, Hangchow, and Shao-hsing maintained their technical advance throughout the Han dynasty. Shortly after the collapse of the empire, they devised a means of firing slightly ferruginous glazes under reducing conditions. The ware thus obtained has passed into history as "Old Yüeh."

(*A*) This animal has the noble pose of contemporary or slightly later tomb guardians, but, in conformity with the still lingering Han spirit, it is shown in crouching position with almost pitiful stump legs.

(*B*) Stone counterparts are known to have been in existence as early as the third century A.D. The frog on top of the lid was a small water container, and the ink was mixed on the tray. The incised details of the frog, as well as the stamped rows of circles and lozenges on the lid, have the crispness characteristic of Southern pieces.

(*C*) This small jar with its uneven grayish olive-green glaze, its depressed body, its tall neck equipped with four slightly "pinched" loop handles, and its flat reddish base is an example of the technically most successful group of early "Old Yüeh."

(*D*) In parallel with their "reduced" wares, Yüeh potters of the Six Dynasties also developed some oxidized vessels with a yellowish tint and a decoration of iron-brown spots. This is the first departure from strictly monochrome glazes.

C.

B.

D.

A.

PLATE XV

TIGER JAR, Glazed Stoneware

Western Chin dynasty
(265–316 A.D.)
Yüeh type
H: 9″ D: 11″   B65P37
Published: d'Argencé, *op. cit.*, p. 93, Pl. IV

"Old Yüeh" has a distinctive olive-green tint and a slightly oily touch which
foreshadows the texture of so many bluish-green glazes of later periods and more
immediately that of the classical Sung celadons.

Yüeh potters of the Western Chin and other Southern dynasties frequently
incorporated derivations of Han animal shapes in their vessels. At times the process is
reversed and a traditional animal shape is hollowed out to make a convenient
container. This syncretic approach so far had been followed more by
bronze-casters than by potters.

The shoulder of this large jar is adorned with a tiger's head on one side and the
embryo of a tail on the other. Although the animal head is fully modeled with its
mouth wide open, it is not functional for it does not communicate with the inside
of the vessel. The sturdy loop handles set in axial position are impressed with
geometric motifs. The base is concave. As a result of technical difficulties common to
all experimental stages, the glaze stops short of the foot where it runs in uneven streaks.

PLATE XVI

A. BACTRIAN CAMEL, Painted Pottery

Wei period
(First part of 6th Century A.D.)
Northern type
H: 9¾″ W: 8½″   B60P309

B. WARRIOR, Painted Pottery

Wei period
(First part of 6th Century A.D.)
Northern type
H: 7¾″   B60P1630

C. CHIMERA, TOMB GUARDIAN, Painted Pottery

Wei period
(First part of 6th Century A.D.)
Northern type
H: 12½″ D: 8″   B60P331

For more than two centuries, successive waves of foreign influences had rolled over
Wei territories to blend with well-established Han traditions, and the first part of
the sixth century marks the appearance of a new type of funerary statuary in North
China. Frequently modeled from common clay, planted on flat rectangular bases, and
hastily painted with brilliant but volatile pigments, these figurines can hardly be
regarded as technical improvements. Their appeal resides primarily in subject matters
and structural innovations. When Han grave figurine-makers and their immediate
successors had concentrated on farm and village scenes, the Wei seem to be fascinated
by long journeys across the deserts of Central Asia. Their taste has become
cosmopolitan. Furthermore, they always appear to be on the lookout for the most
diverting aspect of their models and rarely miss it.

(A) Proportion and posture have been carefully studied to create a striking effect.
Just packed, the camel is now rising on its legs with its head lifted up to help in
the effort. The woolly neck is enormous; the head comparatively small but very alert,
the legs so skinny they seem unfit to carry such an imposing mass.

(B) This warrior wears the long coat, baggy trousers, and helmet of a lancer. The
pug nose, round eyes, arched eyebrows, and abundant beard are a frequent caricature of
a Western face.

(C) With the Wei, the habit of placing such fantastic creatures in tombs became
commonplace. Although their identity is still under discussion, they have been
called "earth spirits," "demons," or "tomb guardians," and are supposed to embody
vicious spirits whose main function would be to guard the tomb from evil influences.

A.

B.

C.

PLATE XVII

A. YOUNG OFFICIAL, Glazed Pottery

Sui or Early T'ang dynasty
(Late 6th to Early 7th Century A.D.)
H: 24½"   B60P118+
Published: d'Argencé, *op. cit.,* p. 95, fig. 26

B. AMPHORA, Glazed Stoneware

Sui or Early T'ang dynasty
(Late 6th to Early 7th Century A.D.)
H: 18½" D: 10"   B60P1143

C. AMPHORA, Black-Glazed Stoneware

Sui or Early T'ang dynasty
(Late 6th to Early 7th Century A.D.)
H: 13" D: 6½"   B60P148

The first colored glazes to follow the traditional olive-green surface of Yüeh origin were a transparent straw-colored yellow and a rich brownish black. Both seem to have originated during the short-lived but momentous Sui dynasty. Sui potters should also be credited with stylistic innovations affecting pottery as well as clay statuary and opening the way to T'ang imperial art. Sui pieces are frequently large, robust, and dignified; they blend strength, elegance, and fancy into an unprecedented formula whose freshness and vigor are symptomatic of a new movement. The time is not far when ceramics will reach such a degree of sophistication that they will be regarded as worthy to grace the imperial table.

(A) Hard-fired grayish white ware with thick straw-colored glaze showing an intricate network of fine crackles.

The ceremonial garment of this young civil official of Mongol or Turkish stock consists of a pillow-shaped hat, a long robe, and a leather waistcoat. The statuette stands on a circular socle which occupies an intermediate position between earlier slabs and rock-shaped T'ang pedestals.

(B) and (C) This type of funeral amphora occupies a prominent place among the numerous category of vessels showing marked Western influences. It was readily accepted by T'ang potters but not without undergoing a number of alterations and additions in line with the usual ponderous and standardizing T'ang approach. Our examples have bulging ovoid bodies, small bases, slender necks surmounted by cup-shaped mouths with everted rims. The bow-shaped handles have circular applied medallions and terminate in crested dragon heads biting the lips of the vessels. In both cases, glazes ran short of the foot. The neutral or straw-colored one has been applied over a white slip.

C.

A.

PLATE XVIII

A. COVERED JAR, Green-Glazed Stoneware

T'ang dynasty
(8th to 9th Century A.D.)
H: 12" D: 11"   B60P279

B. JAR, Black-Glazed Stoneware

T'ang dynasty
(8th to 9th Century A.D.)
H: 8½" D: 8"   B60P138

C. EWER, Black-Glazed Stoneware

T'ang dynasty
(8th to 9th Century A.D.)
H: 9½" D: 9"   B60P141

The T'ang period is primarily that of the first great glaze colorists. The accumulated efforts of so many generations of potters are now fully rewarded. A great part of this success is due to the idea of mixing coloring agents obtained from metallic oxides to such lead-silicate glazes as were known already in Han time. In less than three generations T'ang potters will not only master all kinds of monochrome applications, but will also find the way to decorate the same object with two or three different colors. T'ang colors are at once rich, brilliant, and deep, thus producing a lustrous, warm effect which is unique in the history of Chinese ceramic art and has largely contributed to an early popularity among Western collectors (see Pl. XXIII and cover). Simultaneously, T'ang shapes and decor frequently reflect a new wave of central Asian and near-eastern influences which are perhaps best exemplified by contemporary metalcraft (see *Bronze Handbook* Pl. LIX).

As exemplified by the three pieces illustrated here, many T'ang jars and ewers share structural characteristics such as globular bodies with bulging shoulders, flat bases, and out-turned lips with rounded edges. Bases and even part of the feet are generally unglazed. They reveal a buff, smooth, almost satin-like paste which could only be obtained from choice raw materials carefully levigated.

(A) Short cylindrical neck and low, dome-shaped lid with knob. The thick, glassy green glaze seems to have been applied in successive layers and stops short of the base.

(B) The short, slightly constricted neck is flanked by two small loop handles in upright position. The lustrous black glaze also stops short of the base, but in a less casual manner than in the preceding example.

(C) Short spout in shape of a truncated cone and large, bow-shaped strap handle formed of two strands. Such matt, brownish, black, and all-enveloping glazes are generally assigned to northern kilns, especially those of Honan province.

A.

B.

C.

PLATE XIX

A. EWER, Neutral Glaze With Brown Splashes, Stoneware

T'ang dynasty
(7th to 8th Century A.D.)
Southern type
H: 6⅞" D: 5½"   B60P1807

B. JAR, Black Glaze With "Frosted Gray" Splashes, Stoneware

T'ang dynasty
(7th to 8th Century A.D.)
Northern type
H: 8" D: 8½"   B60P1202

These are two specimens of the unusual and, until today, imperfectly recorded two-color wares, with splashed glazes frequently running over molded areas. Apparently, this highly imaginative decoration was adopted early in the dynasty by a number of kilns north and south of the Yangtze River. The location and time of its first appearance are not yet known with certainty, but it undoubtedly occurred simultaneously if not slightly earlier than the more familiar three-color process.

(A) The body is almost cylindrical and terminates in a reinforced foot rim; on one side a sturdy hexagonal spout, on the other a three-stranded handle, and in symmetrical position two small loop handles, also three-stranded. The buff stoneware paste is covered with an olive-green glaze of the Yüeh type, which runs in uncontrolled streaks towards the base. Below the spout and the lateral spouts three molded leaf motifs have been casually splashed over with a thick layer of brown glaze. During the past decade similar vessels have been found repeatedly in the region of Ch'ang-sha (Hunan) which Chinese archaeologists are inclined to think was the main center of production for these wares.

(B) Buff stoneware with matt brown-black glaze of the so-called Honan type. Two molded floral motifs on the shoulder. Large areas on the upper part of the vessel and inside the everted lip are covered with superimposed "frosted gray" glaze which seems to have been flung over from a distance and as the vessel was still spinning on the wheel. Much later such effects were going to be fully exploited by potters of peripheral areas, notably Korean and Japanese. In China, their success appears to have been limited in time and space.

A.

B.

PLATE XX

A. VASE, Porcelain

T'ang dynasty
(8th to 9th Century A.D.)
so-called "Hsing-yao" type
H: 9½" D: 5"   B60P394

B. CUP, Porcelain

T'ang dynasty
(8th to 9th Century A.D.)
so-called "Hsing-yao" type
H: 2¾" D: 3¾"   B60P216

C. SMALL PLATE WITH FOLIATED RIM, Porcelain

T'ang dynasty
(8th to 9th Century A.D.)
so-called "Hsing-yao" type
H: 1⅛" W: 5⅜"   B60P1392

According to a long-standing tradition, eighth century potters working at a Hsing-chou (Hopei) kiln were able to produce a white ware "with the consistence of silver and the texture of snow," This kiln has not yet been identified, but its name is frequently mentioned in association with a variety of fine pre-Sung porcelaneous wares. The objects shown here seem to fall in this category. They resemble closely pieces which have been published by distinguished experts as plausible "Hsing-yao."

(A) White porcelain with a creamy glaze. The ovoid body is divided into four lobes by deep vertical grooves. On each side are two three-stranded slots, probably for the passage of carrying straps.

(B) One of a group of four cups. The complete set consisted of five cups with a three-legged tray. White porcelain partly covered with a crazed creamy white glaze. These shapes have an almost metallic precision with very thin walls, sharp mouth rims and small spreading feet with beveled rim.

(C) This small plate could serve as an illustration of the famous allusion to "silver and snow." It has the unctuous whiteness of the latter and its shape and floral design are borrowed from middle to late T'ang metalcraft. The base, unglazed, is slightly concave and seems to have been somewhat distorted during the firing.

A.

C.

B.

PLATE XXI

A. T'IEN-WANG (LOKAPALA), Tomb Guardian, Painted Pottery

T'ang dynasty
(680–750 A.D.)
H: 21⅛"   B62S60

B. HORSE AND RIDER, Painted Pottery

T'ang dynasty
(680–750 A.D.)
H: 14⅛"   B64P7

Pursuing a course initiated shortly after the downfall of the Han, T'ang grave goods makers concentrated on the manufacture of vessels and statuettes. The taste discussed in connection with the Six Dynasties is now fully consecrated. Architectural models and bucolic scenes become exceedingly rare, courtly, military, and exotic subjects increase in number and quality. No other single branch of T'ang art reflects more vividly the spirit of the time, the splendor of the capital, the pleasures of the well-to-do, the might of the T'ang army, the far-reaching authority of the T'ang rule, and the deep-reaching, although frequently suppressed influence of Buddhism.

(A) Such guardians borrowed from the Buddhistic pantheon came to supplement the traditional chimerae (Pl. XVI). Standing on a rock, a bull or a demon, they are usually clad in full T'ang armor of the middle period.

(B) This horseman, like the preceding warrior, has Western features. A variety of figurines with the same exaggerated nose, abundant beard, and cap, have been described as representative of the Uighur or Sogdian race.

A.

B.

PLATE XXII

A. GIRL ATTENDANT, Painted Pottery

T'ang dynasty
(First part of 8th Century A.D.)
H: 14"   B60P305

B. and C. MUSICIANS, Painted Pottery

T'ang dynasty
(First part of 8th Century A.D.)
H: 7½"   B60P 317 and 318
Published: d'Argencé, *op. cit.,* p. 93, Pl. III

T'ang statuary potters seem to work from nature more than their predecessors. In this last great moment of funerary sculpture, realism in the Western sense of the word tends to replace the notional approaches of former ages. For the first time, perhaps, bodies are the subject of much attention. Well-proportioned, fully three-dimensional, and dynamic, they are now treated not as mere supports or channels, but as features as essential as the masks themselves. Technically, two types of funerary sculpture are distinguishable. The more numerous (illustrated here and on the preceding plate) is made from common, although carefully mixed clay, frequently covered with a white slip and decorated with multi-color pigments.

T'ang women apparently solved, at least temporarily, a crucial and eternal problem by setting two opposite standards of feminine beauty: the one represented here is probably acceptable to anyone; the other one is illustrated by a numerous series of dignified and emphatically plump ladies whom today we might be tempted to call just fat.

One of the musicians plays a string instrument, the ancestor of the modern ch'in and koto. A standard T'ang orchestra comprised several types of string instruments, flutes, drums, cymbals and castanets.

A.

B.

C.

PLATE XXIII

A. GROOM, Three-Colored Glazes, Pottery

> T'ang dynasty
> (680–750 A.D.)
> H: 23"   B60P536

B. BACTRIAN CAMEL, Three-Colored Glazes, Pottery

> T'ang dynasty
> (680–750 A.D.)
> H: 35"   B60S95

The arduous problem of applying various coloring agents to the same feldspar glaze was at least partly solved early in the T'ang dynasty.

(A) Camel drivers and grooms are frequently represented with Altaic features and garments. This one has a half-comical, half-roguish expression. His brown tunic with green lapels and his partly unglazed boots are of east Iranian type. The face, unglazed, still shows traces of mineral pigments. The long thick hair is arranged in a braided chignon which goes from ear to ear. Originally the clenched fists held a rope.

(B) During the time of intensive traffic along the desert avenues of the old Silk Road, it was only logical that camels should be a subject of sculpture second only to horses. Many camels are rendered with an almost caricatural realism but few attain such proportions or intense vitality. A slightly smaller but otherwise similar animal was discovered in a tomb of a high court official who died in 728 A.D. When describing this animal, the eminent British specialist William H. Honey noted that "it would be found no less impressive as a work of art, as an ordered rhythmical complex of curved and angular surfaces if we did not know that it is a closely observed and 'life-like' rendering of that singular beast."

The pack-saddle consists of a cloth with two holes for the humps, and frames in lattice work support some useful objects including a jug, a gourd, a large piece of meat, a blanket, and a sack decorated with large monster masks which leave no doubt as to the funerary function of the piece.

The potter, anxious to convey the feeling of an animal in motion, paid particular attention to the shaping of the base while making it as inconspicuous as possible.

A.

B.

PLATE XXIV

A. and B. PAIR OF CHIMERAE, (Tomb Guardians) Three-Colored Glazes, Pottery

T'ang dynasty
(680–750 A.D.)
H: 38"   B60S51+ and 52+
Published: Trubner, *op. cit.,* p. 73, No. 160

These ferocious monsters are further examples of the time-honored and diversified tomb guardians (Pls. XVI, XXI) whose function was to protect the tomb from evil influences.

The size of this pair indicates that it was made for a person of high rank. They were placed on either side of the entrance of the burial chamber. Like all Buddhist guardians and lions of the period, these hybrid creatures are set on a high rock-shaped pedestal. However, unlike their human counterparts they are usually sitting in menacing immobility.

(A) The origin of this beast can be traced back to at least the Warring States period. Since Han times it was known as P'i-hsieh (literally "wards off evil"). It is a composite beast with the horns and feet of a deer, the head and body of a lion, a pair of wings, and a huge flame.

(B) This is a newcomer among the tomb guardians. Hybrids with human heads were introduced rather late in the Six Dynasties. In keeping with the cosmopolitan spirit prevailing during the T'ang, this face looks like the caricature of some Western Asian caravan traveler. The head gear resembles a high conical felt hat of Sassanian origin.

This "guardian" is hornless, but has a pair of ears of gigantic dimensions. This might indicate that his primary function was to discover distant danger, and to warn the other guardian.

B.   A.

PLATE XXV

A. HORSE, Three-Colored Glazes, Pottery

T'ang dynasty
(680–750 A.D.)
H: 14⅜″ L: 18″   B60P22+
Published: d'Argencé, *op. cit.,* p. 97, Pl. V

B. GOOSE-SHAPED VESSEL, Three-Colored Glazes, Pottery

T'ang dynasty
(680–750 A.D.)
H: 12″ L: 13⅞″   B60P1108
Published: Trubner, *The Arts of the T'ang Dynasty*
No. 213

C. WINE PEDDLER, Three-Colored Glazed Pottery

T'ang dynasty
(680–750 A.D.)
H: 13¼″   B60P521
Published: Trubner, *op. cit.,* No. 171,
d'Argencé, *Apollo,* Aug. 1966, p. 98, fig. 31
and *Asia Foundation Program Bulletin,*
Special Issue, Aug. 1966, Pl. V

In many instances human masks were left unglazed to be carefully
painted with mineral pigments over a white slip. As well exemplified here, saddles
can also receive the same treatment. These painted areas have lost much of their lustre
but what is left of them seems to indicate that they were originally focal points in
the decoration.

(*A*) Horses form the most numerous animal series. When represented alone they
can be with or without saddle and are shown in all kinds of positions although the
most typical posture is the one illustrated here where the legs are firmly planted in the
ground and the head turned sideways. The outstanding characteristic of this example
is the profuse use of cobalt blue in the coat.

(*B*) Animal-shaped vessels and also rhytons are common during the T'ang period,
but this is a rare shape. One of its distinctive features is the blending of realism
(as expressed by the general contours) and abstraction (as in the treatment of the
spiraling tail and streamlined wings). For practical reasons the feet are generally
omitted in the bird-shaped containers. The lid, now lost, was in the shape of a lily pad
with a knob resembling a diminutive toad. (See also cover)

(*C*) T'ang male figurines often reflect a predilection for exotic types. (See also Pl.
XXI.) The Han were mostly interested in their own simple environment and activities,
but the T'ang prefer to observe the dignitaries of the regime or the strange "barbarians"
who came from all corners of the world to visit Ch'ang-an, the capital.

A.

C.

B.

PLATE XXVI

A. THREE-LEGGED FOLIATED TRAY, Three-Colored Glazes, Pottery

T'ang dynasty
(680–750 A.D.)
H: 2⅛" D: 11"   B60P524
Published: d'Argencé, *op. cit.*, p. 96, fig. 30

B. BIRD-HEADED EWER, Three-Colored Glazes, Pottery

T'ang dynasty
(680–750 A.D.)
H: 13¼" W: 7"   B60P214
Published: d'Argencé, *op. cit.*, p. 96, fig. 29

C. CANDLESTICK, Three-Colored Glazes, Pottery

T'ang dynasty
(680–750 A.D.)
H: 19"   B60P535
Published: Trubner, *op. cit.*, fig. 192
d'Argencé, *op. cit.*, p. 96, fig. 28

The bulk of T'ang three-color grave goods consists of a wide variety of household
vessels, cups, bowls, dishes, platters, trays, jugs, ewers, vases, lamps, and so on.

As in the series of T'ang figurines, shapes and decorative motifs frequently show
signs of foreign influence.

Only when the potter decorated flat surfaces was he able to avoid overlapping of the
various coloring agents. This was achieved through deep incisions separating the
colors and serving as drains or by the use of previously stained glazes. These processes
were so demanding and limitative that, on the whole, they were restricted to trays,
dishes, plates, or boxes which all present horizontal planes. In other cases, potters
let their colors run more or less freely thus creating mottled and streaked effects. The
most usual colors are orange, brown, yellow, green, and blue obtained from red
earth, iron, copper, and cobalt.

Pastes—white, buff, or rosy—vary from earthenware to stoneware quality but are
frequently refined to a satin-like finish.

(A) This rare specimen imitates silver wares of Byzantine or near-eastern inspiration.
In most specimens of this type the number of leaves is restricted to four and designs
do not show much metallic precision.

(B) The shape, the motifs of phoenixes and formal foliage, on one side, and of a
Parthian horseman on the other, and also the relief work suggesting embossing,
all point to a Sassanian model in bronze or silver.

(C) In this specimen the potter relied on simple, traditional shapes and abstract
decorative effects resulting from an astute arrangement of the coloring agents.

B.

C.

A.

PLATE XXVII

A. VASE, Green-Glazed Pottery

Liao dynasty
(907–1126 A.D.)
H: 13″   B60P1103
Published: d'Argencé, *op. cit.*, p. 99, fig. 34

B. EWER, Green-Glazed Pottery

Liao dynasty
(907–1126 A.D.)
H: 6¼″ D: 5¼″   B60P1620
Published: Trubner, *op. cit.*, fig. 279

C. EIGHT-LOBED PLATE, Three-Colored Glazes, Stoneware

Liao dynasty
(907–1126 A.D.)
D: 5⅜″ H: 1⅜″   B60P1551
Published: d'Argencé, *op. cit.*, p. 101, Pl. VI

D. THREE-LEGGED STAND, Three-Colored Glazes, Pottery

Liao dynasty
(907–1126 A.D.)
H: 3¾″ D: 5¾″   B60P215
Published: d'Argencé, *op. cit.*, p. 101, Pl. VIII

With the exception of monkey or bird silhouettes and monster masks Liao potters neglect animal art and concentrate on floral motifs. In spite of imaginative color combinations, their palette is poorer than that of the T'ang. Blue glazes are exceedingly rare.

(A) There are two main groups of tall, slender vases, one with trumpet-like mouths, the other with cup-shaped mouths frequently crowning a bird's head. The former, illustrated here, is the simpler of the two. Such vases usually bear no other decor than a monochrome glaze over a white slip.

(B) The molded designs on this pear-shaped vessel are unusual. Arranged geometrically around the body are various kinds of sea-shells like so many fanciful flowers. The glaze is uniformly green with the exception of a dark spot high on the shoulder. The lid is similar to those of saddle gourds (See next plate).

(C) A number of small dishes, trays, stands and saucers bear pressed or molded floral designs covered with multicolor glazes. Frequently the pigments have been applied so casually that the crispness of the pattern is lost under a maze of blotches.

(D) The half-human, half-animal masks are supported without transition by feline paws, thus combining what used to be in T'ang metalcraft two separate motifs (See *Bronze Handbook* Pl. LVIII).

A.

D.

C.

B.

PLATE XXVIII

A. SADDLE-GOURD, Iridescent Glaze, Pottery

Liao dynasty
(907–1126 A.D.)
H: 9" W: 5¼" B60P1388

B. SADDLE-GOURD, Green-Glazed Pottery

Liao dynasty
(907–1126 A.D.)
H: 9" B60P1106
Published: Trubner, *op. cit.*, fig. 276

C. SADDLE-GOURD, Iridescent Glaze, Pottery

Liao dynasty
(907–1126 A.D.)
H: 10¾" B60P529
Published: Trubner, *op. cit.*, fig. 275
d'Argencé, *op. cit.*, fig. 36

The Liao dynasty kept T'ang traditions alive in the northern provinces for more than two centuries. Much of their production was conservative, but they also conceived shapes and decorative motifs which reflected their nomadic origins and are frequently suggestive of metal or leatherwork.

This is perhaps the most distinctive and original group in Liao pottery. Saddle gourds, also known as leather bottles, were not suggested by T'ang prototypes. They duplicate in ceramic a piece of equipment indispensable to all nomadic people.

Saddle gourds were made in various shapes and designs. Some remain close to the leather models and hardly have foot or base. (A) Others have been practically converted into a vessel by a sturdy and often slightly splaying foot encircling a recessed base (B and C). Some have necks provided with a deep notch to insure a better grip, and two perforations serving as suspension holes (A), and some are equipped with elaborate sculptured handles (B).

Part of the design, usually in molded form, suggests the seams or trappings of the original leather bags. Otherwise bodies can be quite plain (C) or freely incised with more or less conventionalized floral patterns (A and B).

As shown in our examples A and C, the green glazes of buried items frequently take on an iridescence reminiscent of that discussed in connection with the Han grave goods (Pls. IX-C X-A).

C.

B.

A.

PLATE XXIX

A. CEREMONIAL VASE, Celadon, Porcelaneous Stoneware

Five dynasties or Early Sung period
(10th Century A.D.)
"Gray Ware" of Yüeh type
H: 15¾" D: 8" B60P7+

B. EWER, Celadon, Porcelaneous Stoneware

Five dynasties or Early Sung period
(10th Century A.D.)
"Gray Ware" of Yüeh type
H: 6½" B60P2380
Published: d'Argencé, *op. cit.*, p. 102, fig. 37

C. PLATE, Olive-Green Glaze, Porcelaneous Stoneware

Late T'ang or Five Dynasties
(9th to 10th Century A.D.)
D: 5⅝" B62P173

The tenth century marked the official recognition of Yüeh celadons. Not just locally at the court of the Ch'ien rulers, but nationwide, since, as early as 960 and until 1068, the first emperors of the Sung dynasty received an annual contingent of the celebrated Pi-ssu ware.

This is the last step before full-fledged porcelain. Links with the past are more stylistic than technical, for many of these wares already have the density and degree of vitrification of mature Sung porcelains.

Figures *A* and *B* illustrate the "gray ware" which distinguishes itself by very light gray paste, the presence of two small loops on the shoulder, and frequently the division of the bodies into vertical panels. The bluish or greenish glaze is usually very pale.

(*A*) The body is hexagonal. Each panel is framed by bamboo-like poles surmounted by human masks. The upper part of these panels forms a niche occupied by a Buddhist figure seated on a high pedestal. The foot, also, is hexagonal. The elaborate cover represents a lotus bud in openwork rising from a dome in the shape of large petals. The decoration is partly applied, partly molded, and partly incised.

(*B*) Cup-shaped mouth, slender neck with three horizontal grooves toward the base, six-paneled body, and shallow, spreading foot. The enormous spout and handle have been molded in a casual way.

(*C*) Shang-lin-hu (Yü-yao) products are noted for the quality of their glaze and the fineness of their incised decoration. They are considered to be among the most sophisticated celadons of the period, and certain authors associate them with the Pi-ssu ware mentioned above.

A.

B.

C.

PLATE XXX

A. EWER, Porcelaneous Stoneware, Olive-Green Glaze

Sung dynasty
(11th to 12th Century A.D.)
Northern Celadon (possibly from Yao-chou)
H: 9" D: 6½"   B60P1233
Published: W. Honey, *The Ceramic Art of China
and Other Countries in the Far East*, Pl. 37A

B. CUP STAND, Porcelaneous Stoneware, Olive-Green Glaze

Sung dynasty
(11th to 12th Century A.D.)
Northern Celadon
H: 7" W: 7"   B60P1379
Published: H. Garner, *Sung and Later Ceramic Wares*,
p. 128, fig. 1

C. FLOWER HOLDER, Porcelaneous Stoneware, Olive-Green Glaze

Sung dynasty
(11th to 12th Century A.D.)
Northern Celadon
H: 2⅜" D: 5½"   B60P1758

During the eleventh and twelfth centuries Yüeh ideals and techniques were carried on by a number of northern kilns, some of them sponsored by the court itself. Robust yet elegant, frequently carved, combed or impressed with floral or animal designs, and covered with moiré glazes showing a wide range of shades from deep olive-green to yellowish-brown, these wares are commonly known in the West under the generic term of Northern Celadons. Japanese specialists have used that of Ju ware since it was proved that Ju-chou, in southern Honan, was one of the most advanced centers of production of "northern celadons." Here again, however, the results obtained by Chinese archaeologists during the past fifteen years or so throw considerable new light on the subject. These vague terminologies may soon be replaced by more precise ones.

(A) The globular body ends in a tall, cylindrical neck widening toward the mouth. The two-stranded handle makes a right angle just before reaching the neck. The spout is coarsely modeled and slightly off-center. A carved design of chrysanthemum scrolls occupies the front part of the body.

(B) The base and part of the stem are reticulated. The dome-shaped mouth rim is decorated with a carved scroll of peony leaves.

(C) This deep bowl has a projecting mouth rim and an outside design of carved petals. Inside the rim are six groups of three molded tubular holders. Rising from the center is a reticulated dome with perforations alternately circular and leaf-shaped. Such containers have been found standing on top of stands similar to the one in (B).

B.   A.   C.

PLATE XXXI

A. INCENSE BURNER IN SHAPE OF BRONZE TING, Olive-Green Glaze, Porcelaneous Stoneware

Sung Dynasty
(11th to 12th Century A.D.)
Northern Celadon (Yao-chou type)
H: 6⅞" D: 7½"   B60P13+

B. CEREMONIAL JAR, Olive-Green Glaze, Porcelaneous Stoneware

Northern Sung dynasty
(10th to 11 Century A.D.)
Li-shui type (Chekiang)
H: 15½" D: 7½"   B60P151

C. EWER, Olive-Green Glaze, Porcelaneous Stoneware

Sung dynasty
(10th to 13th Century A.D.)
Yüeh type
H: 9¾"   B66P12

As indicated before, (Pls. XXIX, XXX) early during the Sung dynasty, potters working both north and south of the Yangtze river vied in perfecting celadons of the Yüeh type. A comparison of these three vessels shows that this "nationwide" effort produced different results according to the geographical location of the various kilns.

(A) This incense burner is one of the typical "Northern Celadons" as illustrated on the preceding plate. To my knowledge, no similar piece has ever been excavated intact. Both the overlapping tiers of carved petals of the neck and the carved lotus scroll of the body are practically identical with those appearing on shards recently unearthed at the Yao-chou kilns near T'ung-ch'uan in Shensi province.

Note also the legs in the form of feline masks with combed manes over tigers' paws (Pl. XVII-D).

(B) This jar is distinguished from the standard "Northern Celadons" by a lack of craftsmanship, which shows in the potting and the casual appearance of the "scraped base." Such vessels were probably made in southern Chekiang.

(C) Here the difference is more striking. The carved floral design is rather disorganized. The paste and rough glaze remain close to those of the tenth-century "gray ware" of Yüeh-type (Pl. XXIX). In this example, Yüeh potters may have introduced new "northern celadon" ornamental schemes in local traditional items.

A.

B.

C.

PLATE XXXII

PILLOW, White-Glazed Porcelain

Sung dynasty
(11th to 12 Century A.D.)
Ting ware (Hopei)
H: 6″ L: 7½″   B60P1351
Published: Garner, *op. cit.*, p. 129, fig. 2

Kilns in the vicinity of Ting-chou, in central Hopei, enjoyed the patronage of the
Northern Sung rulers and reached their highest degree of excellence in the first quarter
of the twelfth century, during the reign of Hui-tsung. (See also Pls. XXXIII and
XXXIV.) Later, after the "passage to the South," several southern kilns imitated the
ware.

A baby reclining on a rectangular couch upholds a large fungus. Edges of both the
plant and the base of the couch are scalloped. On the vertical sides of the base are
freely incised grooves suggesting tapestry folds. The cap of the fungus, forming
a head-rest, is decorated with a carved pattern of floral scroll.

Kao Lien, a late Ming writer, thought highly of this type of pillows which he
described in his *Eight Discourses on the Art of Living* published in 1591.

PLATE XXXIII

BOWL, Creamy-Glazed Porcelain

Sung dynasty
(11th to 12th Century A.D.)
Ting ware (Hopei)
H: 6″ D: 12½″   B60P1491

Except for a slight ivory tint in the glaze, most Ting ware would fit the demanding
Western definition of porcelain. Bodies are usually pure white, hard, resonant, and
translucent. The glaze, very thin, contains "tear drops" or "droplets." These wares were
baked upside down so that frequently the bases are glazed but the mouth rim bare
or bound in metal bands (Pl. XXXIII). Designs are carved with a hard point, molded,
or stamped. All wares show floral and animal motifs, some also shapes and
geometrical patterns borrowed from ancient bronze art.

This is one of the largest Ting bowls in existence. The inside is incised with a subtle
and parsimonious design of floral scrolls, the outside is ribbed and decorated with
three tiers of incised lotus petals. The base is unglazed and the mouth rim encased in
a copper band.

PLATE XXXIV

A. BOWL, Creamy-Glazed Porcelain

Sung dynasty
(11th to 12th Century A.D.)
Ting ware (Hopei)
D: 9½"   B60P1661

B. EIGHT-LOBED PLATE, Creamy-Glazed Porcelain

Sung dynasty
(11th to 12th Century A.D.)
Ting ware (Hopei)
D: 8½"   B60P1393

C. PLATE, Creamy-Glazed Porcelain

Sung dynasty
(11th to 12th Century A.D.)
Ting ware (Hopei)
D: 9"   B60P1404

The collection contains a wide selection of table wares which formed the bulk of the production of Ting-chou kilns. These three specimens show that Ting potters usually managed to introduce a personal touch even in the most "mechanized" of their products.

Our pieces also show that the designs conceived by Ting potters were frequently more diversified and compact than those of other Sung wares, with the exception of the Tz'u-chou wares (Pls. XXXVII to XL).

(A) This deep bowl exemplifies the simplest and also most free type of decoration: bold floral scrolls are incised all over the available surface without any sectionalism or even evident composition.

(B) Here, despite a marked contrast between the plain rim and the densely decorated bottom, a kind of "vegetal unity" was achieved through a subtle transition from the scalloped rim to the impressed design of mixed floral motifs. The plate suggests the open corolla of a flower.

(C) Incised and molded patterns blend here. In the center a peacock stands on a withered branch amidst flowers and foliage. This central scene is enclosed in a raised five-foil frame decorated with a continuous floral scroll. There are two more concentric patterns on the periphery of the bottom: a floral scroll which echoes the one on the frame and a border of classical meanders. The concave sides bear a band of of conventionalized four-petaled motifs; the narrow rim is incised with a scroll pattern, whose fluidity contrasts with the rest of the decor.

A.

B.

C.

PLATE XXXV

MEI-P'ING VASE, Blue and Purple Glaze, Stoneware

Late Sung or Yüan dynasty
(13th to 14th Century A.D.)
Chün ware (Honan)
H: 14" D: 6½"   B60P19+
Published: Garner, *op. cit.,* p. 127, Pl. XIII

Faced by conflicting criteria for dating Chün wares, experts are now awaiting further
archaeological research. This is understandable because in the course of the past
fifteen years or so the Chinese spade has solved many arduous problems which two or
three generations of scholarly debates and speculations had left unanswered.
Two important points have already been established. First, like the best Northern
Celadons and Ting wares, high-quality Chün vessels can be regarded as Court ware
because the kilns which made them were placed under imperial patronage. Second, so
far as Sung Chün ware are concerned the main centers of production hardly exceeded
the limits of the Honan province. A third point, more hypothetical, would be that
complicated shapes and audacious glaze effects are automatically dated after Sung.
Sturdily potted and baked to stoneware hardness, Chün vessels are characterized
by gray bodies, a brown slip on the unglazed base, and bluish thick opalescent glazes
with high phosphatic content. The crimson splashes or suffusions which frequently
enhance the lavender-blue background result from the first attempt on the part of
Chinese potters to take advantage of copper fired under reduced conditions (See
also Pl. XXXVI).

Mei-p'ing or "plum vases" have a slender ovoid body, a short contracted neck, and a
thick projecting lip. The shape conceived by Sung potters was thought to be
particularly suitable for flower arrangements and became popular in subsequent
dynasties.

PLATE XXXVI

A. FLOWER POT, Grey-Blue Glaze, Stoneware

Sung dynasty
(10th to 13th Century A.D.)
Chün ware (Honan)
H: 8¾″   B60P97

B. JARDINIERE, Purple and Blue Glaze, Stoneware

Late Sung or Yüan period
(13th to 14th Century A.D.)
Chün ware (Honan)
H: 6⅜″   B60P18+

C. BULB-BOWL, Purple and Blue Glaze, Stoneware

Late Sung or Yüan period
(13th to 14th Century A.D.)
Chün ware (Honan)
H: 3⅛″ D: 8⅜″   B60P103

D. BOWL, Blue Glaze, Stoneware

Sung dynasty
(10th to 13th Century A.D.)
Chün ware (Honan)
H: 3⅞″ D: 8⅜″   B60P105

Technically Chün wares show some affinity with "Northern Celadons" (Pls. XXX, XXXI-*A* and with the famous, if altogether too rare, Ju-yao, which was also an achievement of Honan kilns. Simultaneously, many Chün shapes echo those of other contemporary productions (*D*). However, one distinctive group of Chün wares consists of large, thick-walled vessels to hold plants and flowers: pots, bulb bowls, jardinières, and so on. Many of these "garden pieces" bear a serial number incised under the slip on the perforated base.

(*A*) The pale-blue glaze, unusually thin, shows "earthworm tracks" in the region of the neck. These are traditionally considered as one of the hallmarks of early Chün ware. In a similarly typical manner, the surface has a pitted appearance due to the presence of innumerable "pin holes" resulting from the bursting of bubbles in the glaze. (See also Pl. XXXV.)

(*B*) and (*C*) The outside of these vessels is suffused with purple producing what is known as flambé effects. Such glazes used to be much appreciated by Western collectors and have largely contributed to the early fame of Chün wares in Europe.

Insides are almost uniformly blue. This contrast is probably due to the fact that inside surfaces were well protected from air draughts in the kiln.

A.

B.

C.

D.

PLATE XXXVII

A. PILLOW, Three-Colored Glaze, Pottery

Sung dynasty
(ca. 11th Century A.D.)
Tz'u-chou ware (Shansi type)
H: 4″ W: 11½″   B60P213

B. BABY, Three-Colored Glaze, Pottery

Late Sung or Yüan period
(13th to 14th Century A.D.)
Tz'u-chou ware
H: 7″   B60P1617

C. BOWL, Marbled Ware

Sung dynasty
(10th to 13th Century A.D.)
Tz'u-chou ware
D: 4¼″   B65P55

D. BOWL, Enameled Ware

Southern Sung dynasty
(12th to 13th Century A.D.)
Tz'u-chou ware
D: 3½″   B60P2387

E. HORSE, Polychrome Glaze, Pottery

Sung dynasty
(10th to 13th Century A.D.)
Tz'u-chou ware
H: 3⅞″   B66P51

(A) The origin of ceramic head rests has been traced back to the T'ang dynasty. During the Sung period they were made in large quantities and in a wide variety of shapes (See also Pl. XL). The main characteristics of this supposedly Shansi type, which retains the flavor of T'ang three-colored wares, are the bean-shaped body made in two halves and an incised decorative motif enclosed in a combed frame.

(B) and (C) Long after the T'ang, the golden age of ceramic figurines, northern potters continued to produce subjects which reflected entirely new tastes and functions. Some of these diminutive and unsophisticated stauettes were made for the scholar's desk or the family altar. Others, like the ones illustrated here, were probably children's toys.

(D) This bowl belongs to a small group which marks the beginnings of enameled decoration on Chinese ceramics.

(E) The technique of mixing two differently colored clays to produce "marbled" or "veined" effects also originated in T'ang times.

A.

B.

C.

D.

E.

PLATE XXXVIII

A.   MEI-P'ING VASE, Stoneware

Sung dynasty
(10th to 13th Century A.D.)
Tz'u-chou type, possibly from Hsiu-wu kilns
H: 19½"   B60P161
Published: Garner, *op. cit.*, p. 131, fig. 5

B.   JAR, Stoneware

Sung dynasty
(10th to 13th Century A.D.)
Tz'u-chou ware (probably from Honan)
H: 8" D: 8½"   B60P197

This numerous category (see also Pls. XXXVII, XXXIX and XL) comprises many
different types commonly known as Tz'u-chou ware in the West, Hsiu-wu ware
in Japan, and Folk ware in China. Beside coming from Tz'-u-chou these wares originate
from a number of kilns in Hopei, Honan, and neighboring provinces. Raw
materials and firing processes are less refined than those of Court wares, shapes suggest
more household furniture than dinner sets, and decorative motifs reflect a dynamism
which contradicts the subdued monochromatic effects of the more sophisticated series.
Here, free from official dictates, potters were able to give full vent to their
imagination; often their products were technically as well as stylistically in advance
of the more formal series. Two major achievements of Sung folk potters —
underglaze-painted decoration and overglaze enamels — set the pattern
of ceramics research for centuries to come.

Kilns centering on Hsiu-wu yao in northern Honan were among the most active and
imaginative of the so-called Tz'u-chou group. Frequently striking decorative effects
were produced by a well-calculated contrast between jet-black and almost pure white
areas.

(A) The overlapping petals at the base of the neck and on the foot are animated
by an anti-clockwise movement; the dense peony scrolls on the body proper are
orientated in the opposite direction. In the graffito method used here, a black slip was
applied over a white one. Then the design was brought to life by scratches and
incisions through the black layer. Finally, the vessel was covered with a neutral gaze.

(B) Here a thick, lustrous black glaze which stops short of the base has been
applied over a white body. The white vertical ribs which show through the glaze are
made of fine threads of applied clay. As might be expected in a country where the
tea ceremony and its paraphernalia occupy such an important place, the current
Japanese school designates such wares as "Honan Temmoku" (Pl. XLVI).

A.

B.

PLATE XXXIX

A. JAR, Painted Stoneware, Neutral Glaze

Sung dynasty
(10th to 13th Century A.D.)
Tz'u-chou ware
H: 8″ W: 8½″   B60P1+
Published: Honey, *op. cit.*, Pl. 72a
Garner, *op. cit.*, p. 129, fig. 3

B. JAR, Painted Stoneware, Neutral Glaze

Sung dynasty
(10th to 13th Century A.D.)
Tz'u-chou ware
H: 6¼″ D: 5½″   B62P169

C. JAR, Stoneware, Cream-Colored Slip and Neutral Glaze

Sung dynasty
(10th to 13th Century A.D.)
Tz'u-chou ware
H: 5½″ W: 6″   B60P131

(*A*) and (*B*) A small but celebrated group of Tz'u-chou-type wares bear floral or leafy designs in brown (*A*) or black (*B*) which can be regarded as typical examples of Sung painting (See also next plate). When they were made in series after set models, they showed individual features that revealed an unprecedented freedom of approach. Here decorators were not mere colorists but trained painters with calligraphic talent. These wares mark the drastic change of taste which occurred in ceramic production during the Sung dynasty. Soon after that time, the entire industry relied primarily on professional painters for decorative effects.

(*C*) By contrast this most "plastic" specimen is covered with five rows of petals in applied relief. Seen from above, the vessel is suggestive of a "heartless" lotus plant. Each petal is strongly modeled, and the glaze which stops short of the base has a matt creamy white tint inspired by that of Ting ware (Pls. XXXII through XXXV). The provenance and usage of such vessels are problematic; they may have been made in Chü-lu hsien in southern Hopei and may have been used in Buddhist ceremonies.

A.

B.

C.

PLATE XL

A. PILLOW, Glazed Stoneware, Black and White Designs

Sung dynasty
(10th to 13th Century A.D.)
Tz'u-chou type
W: 11⅝"   B65P51

B. PILLOW, Glazed Stoneware, Black and White Designs

Sung dynasty
(ca. 11th Century A.D.)
Tz'u-chou type (possibly from Shansi)
H: 4¼" W: 17¼"   B60P421

C. TIGER-SHAPED PILLOW, Glazed Stoneware, Black and White Designs

Late Northern Sung period
(1st quarter of 12th Century A.D.)
Tz'u-chou type
H: 4½" W: 15"   B60P423

After two pillows of Ting and so-called Shansi type (Pls. XXXII and XXXVII), here are three more examples of widely different shapes. They belong to the most numerous group of Tz'u-chou wares decorated in black and white. Chün, Ju, Tung, Yao, and other "Northern Celadon" centers also produced ceramic pillows but, strangely enough, so far no southern sites has yielded any local specimens. Ceramic pillows evidently were made exclusively by northern potters during the Sung period.

(A) Leaf-shaped pillows on a high, hollow, and frequently many-sided stem are uncommon. This one bears an unusual design. The association of a deer and cloud-shaped mushrooms illustrates two ancient beliefs. The deer, a symbol of longevity, was thought to be the only animal capable of finding the sacred fungus of immortality.

Such Taoist emblems of longevity would not appear on a funerary pillow. This and similar allusions to long life or numerous offspring do not support the theory still prevailing in the West that ceramic pillows were made for the dead.

(B) The elongated floral design which adorns the top of this eight-sided pillow has been obtained by using a method similar to the one discussed in connection with the tall vase of Plate XXXVIII, but here the process was reversed (See also the leaf-shaped pillow above).

(C) Until recently anthropomorphic or zoomorphic Tz'u-chou pillows of the painted type were given Late Sung, Yüan, or even later datings. Such attributions may have to be revised. In 1963 the forepart of a pillow very similar to this one was found at Ho-pi-chi, a late Northern Sung kiln site in the northwest of Honan province.

A.

B.

C.

PLATE XLI

INCENSE BURNER, Porcelain

Sung dynasty
(10th to 13th Century A.D.)
Ch'ing-pai type
H: 5¼" D: 4"   B60P1764
Published: Garner, *op. cit.*, p. 131, fig. 4
Royal Academy of Arts, *International Exhibition of
Chinese Art*, p. 936, fig. 940

Characterized by dainty porcelaneous bodies with transparent light-blue glazes, this group belongs to a series of Southern Sung ceramics known in the West as Ying-ch'ing or Ch'ing-pai, although in recent years both Chinese and Japanese scholars have officialized the latter term which appeared already in Sung literature.

Ch'ing-pai ware has been called "the southern counterpart of Ting ware" (Pl. XXXIII). They were produced in great quantities in the southern provinces, especially in Kiangsi, in the region of Ching-te-chen.

Sung potters conceived a variety of shapes and designs borrowed from the vegetal kingdom, and the three specimens shown here illustrate this practice (See also next plate).

The reticulated lid and the plain body form an almost perfect sphere. The upper part of the foot is ringed while the fluted and splaying lower part resembles a corolla.

PLATE XLII

A. JAR, Porcelain

Sung dynasty
(10th to 13th Century A.D.)
Ch'ing-pai type
H: 3¼″ D: 3¾″   B60P117+

B. COSMETIC BOX, Porcelain

Sung dynasty
(10th to 13th Century A.D.)
Ch'ing-pai type
H: 1½″ D: 3″   B60P190

(A) The flat dome-shaped lid is surmounted by a knob and has a foliated rim. The body is lobed with separations marked alternately by grooves and bands of clay in relief. The vessel suggests some kind of cucurbit.

(B) The molded surface bears a grain pattern. Inside three fruit-shaped cups are separated by stems with a flower bud in the center.

A.

B.

PLATE XLIII

CEREMONIAL JAR, Porcelaneous Stoneware

Late Northern Sung period
(ca. 11th Century A.D.)
Lung-ch'üan Celadon
H: 9½" D: 5"   B62P147

Lung-ch'üan celadons are the culmination of a millennial tradition. They saw the light in the Yüeh region, which in ceramic terminology could be called "Celadon Land" (Pls. VIII, IX, XIV, XV, XXIX and XXXI). The internationalization of Lung-ch'üan wares is a Southern Sung achievement (See next plate). We know however, that these kilns were active during the Northern Sung period.

Several specialists, including the most eminent, believe that such altar jars belong to this precocious series.

Barrel-shaped or cylindrical bodies can be plain or decorated with a band of modeled lotus petals which encircles the lower part of the vessel. Shoulders and necks are surrounded by one or several large-headed fierce, gesticulating dragons. Lid knobs are in the form of small, gentle animals, primarily crouching dogs.

Such wares are distinguished from the typical Southern Sung wares by these formal and decorative features and by the unusually thin and smooth glaze.

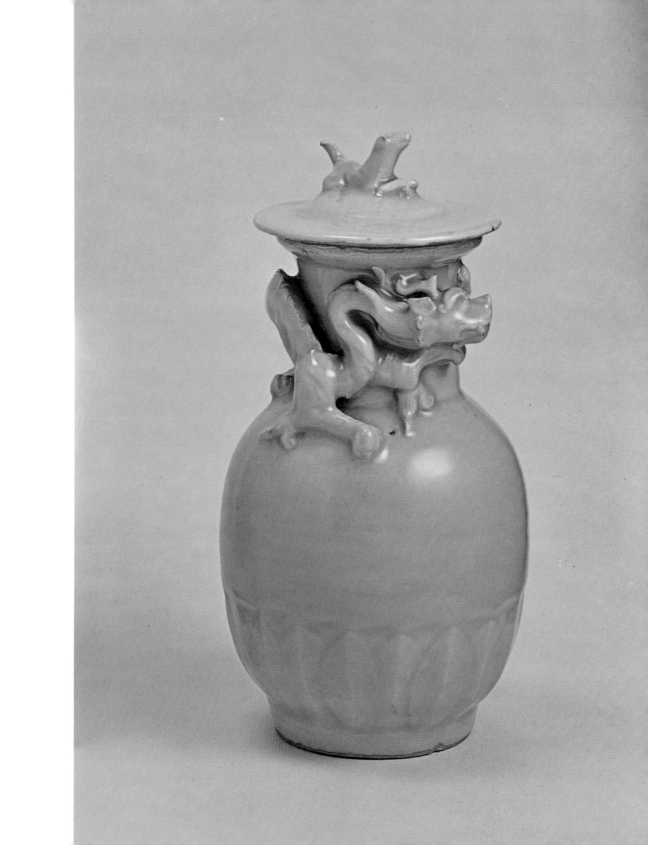

PLATE XLIV

A. TS'UNG-SHAPED VESSEL, Porcelaneous Stoneware

Southern Sung dynasty
(12th to 13th Century A.D.)
Lung-ch'üan Celadon
H: 10″ W: 4″   B60P355

B. HU-SHAPED VASE, Porcelaneous Stoneware

Southern Sung dynasty
(12th to 13th Century A.D.)
Lung-ch'üan Celadon
H: 8¾″ D: 5½″   B60P1483

C. PLATE, Porcelaneous Stoneware

Southern Sung dynasty
(12th to 13th Century A.D.)
Lung-ch'üan Celadon (Tobi Seiji)
D: 6½″   B60P2085

Starting with the Southern Sung, Lung-ch'üan ware became the most popular of all celadons and was exported all over Asia. Bodies are of a gray porcelaneous paste. Glazes are usually thick and glossy. Green or blue-green, they are sometimes extensively crackled. Frequently, enclosed parts have turned reddish-brown during the fire (See also preceding plate).

(A) and (B) Lung-ch'üan shapes are often archaistic thus reflecting the taste which prevailed in scholarly circles of the Sung dynasty. (A) imitates a jade shape which can be traced back to the Han dynasty. (B) has the contours of a bronze vessel of the Late Shang period. (See *Bronze Handbook* Pl. XV.)

(C) This kind of spotted ware is known in Japan under the suggestive term of "flying" or "jumping" celadons (tobi seiji). Like the spots of some old Yüeh ware (Pl. XV-D) these rust-brown marks are due to the oxidization of particles of iron, but here the process has been applied with greater freedom. Care has been taken to avoid symmetric effects.

A.

B.

C.

PLATE XLV

A. JAR, Porcelain

Southern Sung period
(12th to 13th Century A.D.)
Kuan type (Chekiang)
H: 2¼" D: 3¼"   B60P1738

B. OCTAGONAL PLATE, Porcelain

Southern Sung period
(12th to 13th Century A.D.)
Kuan type (Chekiang)
D: 6¼"   B60P2060

C. BOWL, Porcelain

Late Southern Sung or Yüan period
(13th to 14th Century A.D.)
Kuan type (Chekiang)
D: 4⅝"   B62P149

So far, attempts to identify properly the highest levels of ceramic production for the six hundred years from the end of the T'ang period to the beginning of the Yüan dynasty have remained unsuccessful. We mentioned Hsing-yao in connection with the T'ang dynasty, and Pi-ssu yao for the Five Dynasties. The same problem arises regarding Kuan ware of both the Northern and Southern Sung.

The little we know about Southern Kuan ware would indicate that it was made under official control in several kilns in the city of Lin-an (present-day Hang-chou) and its immediate vicinity. By their shapes, their thin and light bodies, their foot rims turned reddish-black during the firing, the loose texture of their lustrous and crackled glazes, and other complementary characteristics such as the sturdiness of their mouth rims, in vivid contrast with the fragility of their feet, our examples seem to answer all requirements listed by the experts.

One of the outstanding peculiarities of this ware is the use of crackles as main decorative motifs. These crackles were produced in a wide variety of lines and colors.

A.

B.

C.

PLATE XLVI

A. BOWL, Stoneware

Sung dynasty
(10th to 13th Century A.D.)
Chien ware (Temmoku)
H: 3" D: 5"   B60P1737

B. BOWL, Stoneware

Sung dynasty
(10th to 13th Century A.D.)
Chien ware (Temmoku)
H: 2¾" D: 7¾"   B60P1718

These two black-glazed tea bowls represent a southern group which became popular in
China and Japan toward the later part of the Sung dynasty with the development
of Ch'an (Zen) tea ceremony, a practice kept alive in Japan to the present day. Somber
glazes have always been preferred by cultists for the pea-green foamy beverage used
in the tea ceremony.
So far the main centers of the so-called Chien or Temmoku ware have been discovered
at Chien-yang and Kuang-tse in Fukien. Chien bowls can be regarded as epitomes
of studied carelessness or, to use a Zen phrase, as "tops of humility." It would be
difficult to find in the history of Oriental ceramics a more successful blending of gravity
and simplicity. Bodies are almost black, and heavily potted. Bases are irregular
as are frequently the general contours. The glazes are thick to the point of making
congealed rolls in the region of the feet, which are generally exposed. Glaze effects such
as the one exemplified in (B) are due to the crystallization of the ferric oxide
contained in the glaze.

A.   B.

PLATE XLVII

A. BOWL, Stoneware

Sung dynasty
(10th to 13th Century A.D.)
Chi-chou ware (Kian)
H: 2" D: 6"   B60P1731

B. BOWL, Stoneware

Sung dynasty
(10th to 13th Century A.D.)
Chi-chou ware (Kian)
H: 2" D: 5½"   B60P176

The term "Kian" formerly applied to this type is now about to be replaced by that of "Chi-chou" as suggested by Chiang Hsüan-t'ai who has recently carried out a thorough investigation of the kilns in question. As a matter of fact, both appelations are but two consecutive names of the same place in Kiangsi.

In some ways the Chi-chou potters were to the Southern Sung what the Tz'u-chou ones had been to the Northern Sung. They specialized in "folk" wares which were frequently inspired by more refined productions. However, they felt free to develop their own type of decor and to indulge in technical experiments which were to contribute to the development of the ceramic art at large.

Rather lightly potted, these bowls are made from buff stoneware covered by a brown slip. They are conical in shape, and their low feet and bases are unglazed and coarse. The button-like projections in the center of the bottoms are a common feature, almost a hall-mark of these wares.

(A) The inside is streaked and mottled with yellow, with sixteen six-petaled flowers "reserved" in black: to produce such effects, sometimes known as "resist" process, potters used paper cut-outs treated in wax or vinegar.

(B) This motif which Chiang Hsüan-t'ai interprets as "plum blossoms in moonlight" was painted in white against a black background.

B.

A.

PLATE XLVIII

A. JAR, Porcelain

Yüan dynasty
(Early 14th Century A.D.)
Ch'ing-pai type
H: 12½" D: 13" B60P48

B. VASE AND STAND, Porcelain

Yüan dynasty
(1280–1368 A.D.)
Ch'ing-pai type
H: 9½" D: 4½" B60P22
Published: Garner, *op. cit.*, p. 131, fig. 5

C. MEI-P'ING VASE, Porcelain

Yüan dynasty
(1280–1368 A.D.)
Lung-ch'üan type
H: 11⅛" D: 6¼" B60P372

These objects illustrate two major changes which took place during the Yüan dynasty. Glazes which had been applied parsimoniously to small, dainty wares were now used freely for large, robust vessels; admittedly losing some of their delicacy in the process. On the other hand, a number of decorative innovations reveal an increasing demand for pictorial effects which so far had been restricted to the lower levels of the ceramic industry. In this sense, many Yüan monochromes can be regarded as blendings of the two main currents prevailing during the Sung dynasty.

(A) A central motif of dragons is framed by a floral scroll on the shoulder and a row of conventionalized lotus petals on the foot. All these patterns are incised.

(B) Pearl-bead decoration originated in the Yüan dynasty when it was mostly associated with Ch'ing-pai glazes. Here this complex device has been used on the vase and its stand.

(C) Each side shows an unglazed panel with one of the Eight Immortals of Taoism in molded relief. This contrasting technique, already used by Lung-ch'üan potters of the late Sung dynasty, was most frequently used during the Yüan and early Ming periods.

A.

C.

B.

PLATE XLIX

A. VASE, Porcelain, Underglaze Red

Yüan dynasty
(1279–1368 A.D.)
Ching-te-chen ware
H: 9½″ D: 5″   B60P1701

B. STEM CUP, Porcelain, Blue and White

Yüan dynasty
(15th Century A.D.)
Ching-te-chen ware
H: 3⅝″ D: 4⅜″   B65P54

Most specialists regard underglaze painted decoration in red or blue as a fourteenth-century innovation. With it, Chinese ceramics enter definitively their pictorial phase.

(A) Two main zones of decoration. On the lower part of the neck vertical arabesques occupy the center of vertical registers. On the body a continuous scroll of floral design. Underglaze red, obtained from copper oxide, is particularly difficult to control and apt to lose its brilliance during the firing. (See also next plate: A). Wholly successful fourteenth- or even fifteenth-century pieces of this type are exceedingly scarce.

Without the striking precedents of the so-called "folk" potters of the Sung period, it would be hard to understand such an involved process associated with a casual brush.

(B) On the outside, a snake-shaped, spiky and three-clawed dragon is chasing a flaming jewel. On the inside of the rim, a border of scrolled tendrils. At the bottom of the cup, a floral motif.

From the standpoint of craftsmanship, this blue and white cup stands in vivid contrast with the underglaze red bottle. Cobalt, from which the blue color was obtained, was rare and expensive, so that this type of decoration was at first almost exclusively restricted to the higher levels of ceramic production. Bodies are closely related to those of the Ch'ing-pai class.

A.

B.

PLATE L

A. VASE, Porcelain, Underglaze Red

Late Yüan or Early Ming dynasty
(14th to 15th Century A.D.)
H: 18″ D: 9″   B60P1235

B. STEM CUP, Blue and White Porcelain

Hsüan Te mark and period
(1426–1435 A.D.)
H: 4″ D: 4″   B60P1512

C. BOWL, Blue and White Porcelain

Hsüan Te mark and period
(1426–1435 A.D.)
H: 2⅞″ D: 6″   B60P2354

D. WINE POT IN SHAPE OF SWIMMING DUCKS, Blue and White Porcelain

Early Ming dynasty
(15th Century A.D.)
H: 4″ L: 5½″   B60P1586

As a rule decorators respected the time-honored tradition according to which each "anatomical" division of a vessel bears a separate decor. This practice led to the adoption of set ornamental schemes for necks, shoulders, and feet. Fourteenth-century and early fifteenth-century vessels, however, frequently show originality even in the treatment of these secondary zones.

(B) and (C) If the shapes of these small containers are well known; their decorative motifs present a number of unusual features. Such are for the stem cup, the zigzag and triangle pattern on the neck and the row of dots on the foot rim. The peripheral zones of the bowl also show uncommon patterns. The main discrepancy, however, are the central bands where almost casual leafy scrolls support or surround formal blossoms.

These naive yet elaborate items create a feeling of freshness rarely found even in blue-and-white wares of the earliest phases.

(D) Mandarin ducks were symbols of conjugal fidelity because of the attachment these beautiful birds show for each other.

The pair has been modeled so as to form one body, and the open beak of one of the birds serves as the spout of the vessel. The base is unglazed.

A.

B.

C.

D.

PLATE LI

A. PLATTER, Blue and White Porcelain

Hsüan Te mark and period
(1426–1435 A.D.)
H: 3⅛″ D: 9″   B60P2101

B. FRUIT BOWL, Blue and White Porcelain

Hsüan Te mark and period
(1426–1435 A.D.)
H: 4″ D: 11″   B60P1662

C. BOWL, Blue and White Porcelain

Ming dynasty
(Early 15th Century A.D.)
H: 3″ D: 14¾″   B65P6

Blue-and-white decoration is considered as having reached its stylistic perfection in the fifteenth century (See also Pls. L and LII).

At that early age, the range of motifs was limited, mostly floral design and dragons, but they often displayed a tempestuous individuality which later was replaced under administrative pressure by more stereotyped arrangements. The habit of painting in splashes with no or little outline was the source of lively and warm effects.

(A) The main motif in the center of this platter consists of three bunches of grapes. On both faces of the sides is a floral band with twelve units of various species. The top of the rim has a wave pattern, which first appeared during the Yüan dynasty. The base is unglazed.

Shiploads of early blue and white porcelains found their way to the western countries of Asia. This piece bears a minute Persian inscription on the foot indicating that it was once in the possession of a Mogul emperor of India.

(B) and (C) The structural characteristics of these items differ greatly. The one is heavily potted; but the other one exhibits a delicacy in texture which is not found in export wares. Such fine pieces were probably made for the Court.

Both bases are glazed. The mark of the stem cup is inside the base within a double circle, a practice which became common in subsequent reigns.

A.

B.

C.

PLATE LII

A. BASIN, Blue and White Porcelain

Early Ming dynasty
(Early 15th Century A.D.)
H: 5½″ D: 12″   B60P33+

B. JAR, Blue and White Porcelain

Early Ming dynasty
(Early 15th Century A.D.)
H: 8½″ D: 10″   B60P245
Published: Garner, *op. cit.*, p. 131, fig. 6

C. MEI-P'ING VASE, Blue and White Porcelain

Ming dynasty
(15th to 16th Century A.D.)
H: 14½″ D: 10″   B60P88

(*A*) and (*B*) These vessels are further examples of the early fifteenth-century blue-and-white production when Near Eastern influence was at its highest. The basin for instance, was made in imitation of Persian metal ware.

The piling of the blue forming blackish blotches in some areas and the presence of numerous tiny dots along the lower edges of outlines are not intentional, but due to impurities in the cobalt. Three centuries later, particularly during the reign of Yung Cheng, these technical defects came to be regarded as marks of excellence and were painstakingly—although not necessarily accurately—imitated (Pl. LXXII).

(C) This is a specimen of a rare white-and-blue series where the usual process is reversed. Here not the design but the background is painted in blue. The body is somewhat softer than usual which accounts for the crackles in the glaze.

C.

B.

A.

PLATE LIII

A. DISH, Blue and White Porcelain

Ming dynasty, Cheng Te mark and period
(1506–1521 A.D.)
D: 9⅛"   B60P1719

B. SEAL BOX, Blue and White Porcelain

Ming dynasty, Chia Ching period
(1522–1566 A.D.)
H: 1¼" D: 4"   B60P1710

Following a tendency that can be traced back to the Sung dynasty, several emperors during the sixteenth-century were largely responsible for the changes in taste which occurred from one generation to the other. This increasing imperial interference is reflected by the now fully systematized practice of marking the pieces made for the Court with a "nien-hao" or reign style.

Usually these marks consist of four or six characters painted in blue under the glaze and frequently enclosed in a frame formed by two concentric circles or squares. The longer inscriptions tell under the reign of which emperor the piece was made, also stating the dynasty. In shorter inscriptions the dynastic title is omitted. Throughout the Ming period these date marks are written with a vigorous if frequently casual brush. Markers tended to favor variations of two calligraphic styles known in Chinese as K'ai (standard) and Li (official).

(A) The first quarter of the century, corresponding to the reign of Cheng Te, is well known for two outstanding series. The so-called Mohammedan group and a category of utensils for the imperial table highly decorated with dragons among floral scrolls.

(B) Chia Ching blue is reputed for the brilliance and homogeneity of its purplish tonality. For the first time the cobalt ore is refined to the point where all impurities are eliminated. Chia Ching themes were influenced by the Taoistic leanings of the reigning monarch (See also next plate). Here, for instance, the pair of phoenixes which appear on top of the lid could be interpreted as an allusion to imperial amorous bliss. The crane is a symbol of longevity; the bird is represented flying and standing on one leg at the outer zone of the cover and on the box itself.

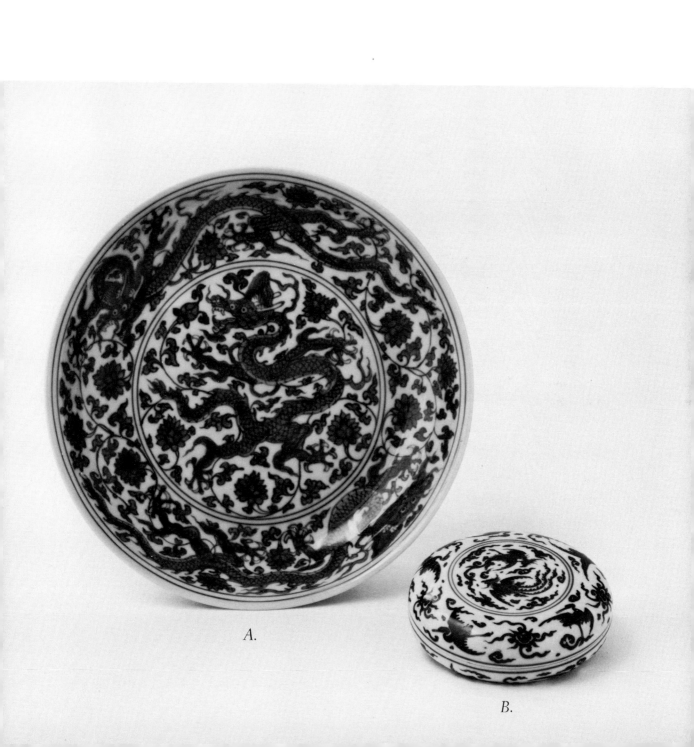

A.

B.

PLATE LIV

POTICHE, Blue and White Porcelain

Mark and period of Chia Ching
(1522–1566 A.D.)
H: 26″ D: 20″   B60P99+

This large storage jar illustrates a typical group of the Chia Ching period. Heavily potted, and consequently usually well preserved, such jars are decorated in the characteristic purple blue with huge, disheveled, spike-spined, and five-clawed sea dragons which seem to be chasing liana-like characters for "longevity." Often the same pattern on a reduced scale occurs on the top and around the vertical side of the lid.

Sea dragons (li) are usually shown without horns.

The date mark on the neck of the vessel is visible when the lid is removed.

PLATE LV

A. SWEET MEAT DISH, Blue and White Porcelain

Wan Li mark and period
(1573–1619 A.D.)
D: 10⅛"   B60P251

B. BOWL, Blue and White Porcelain

Ming dynasty, Wan Li period
(1573–1615 A.D.)
H: 3½" D: 8¼"   B60P261

Toward the end of the Ming dynasty many decorators followed a pictorial and anecdotic trend which had been dormant since at least the later Sung period even though it was then mostly confined to folk wares of the Tz'u-chou type.

In a sense, the late Ming trend can also be regarded as a revival of a Han practice as illustrated by so many tomb vessels showing figures in landscape settings. (See for instance Pl. X.) Both Han and late Ming potters relied heavily on contemporary pictorial art as their main source of inspiration. Here ends the analogy however, for the obvious reason that landscape painting had gone a long way during the some fourteen hundred years which elapsed between the two phenomena.

This late Ming trend set the pattern for the full-fledged story-and-landscape paintings of the Ch'ing period (Pls. LXIX, LXXV). It was encouraged not only by a revival of landscape-painting but also by the enthusiastic response of the European market.

(A) During the later part of the sixteenth-century, imperial kilns remained conservative. If technical changes occurred, they were rarely for the better. The supplies of fine clay in the vicinity of Ching-te-chen had been exhausted in the course of the preceding reigns, and the dearth of adequate raw materials frequently resulted in a lowering of standards.

This box illustrates a theme which painters had made popular as early as the Sung dynasty—children playing in a garden (Pl. XXXII).

(B) "Independent" potters working largely for the foreign market produced in great quantities a ware with many unprecedented features: very thin bodies, no anatomical divisions, and the blue, remarkably pale, applied in a manner which reflects the subtlety of ink monochrome.

B.

A.

PLATE LVI

A. "LOTUS POD" BOWL, White Porcelain

Ming dynasty, Yung Lo period
(1403–1425 A.D.)
H: 3⅜" D: 6⅜"   B60P1705

B. BOX, Bluish White Porcelain

Mark and period of Hsüan Te
(1426–1435 A.D.)
H: 3" D: 6¼"   B60P1594

C. VASE, Porcelain, Turquoise

Ming dynasty, Chia Ching period
(1522–1566 A.D.)
H: 8¼"   B60P1332

D. TEA POT, Stoneware

Ming dynasty
(16th to 17th Century A.D.)
Yi-hsing type
Signed Ch'en Ming-yüan
H: 2" L: 5¼"   B60P2056

Despite a Ming preference for painted wares, high-quality monochromes carried the Sung tradition until the end of the dynasty and beyond.

(A) One outstanding achievement of the first quarter of the fifteenth century is a rare group of "Lien-tzu" or "Lotus Pod" bowls with extremely thin and translucent bodies covered by an almost pure white glaze and bearing a secret (an-hua) decor which is penciled so tenuously that it becomes clearly apparent only when seen against a strong light.

(B) Early Chinese sources emphasize the quality of the white wares of the Hsüan Te period. This covered box with its simple contours, its molded, conventionalized floral decoration, and the slightly greenish tint of its thick lustrous glaze is an example of the kind.

(C) The sixteenth-century, especially the reign of Chia Ching, is noted for the abundance and variety of monochrome glazes. Turquoise is among the new colors of this period.

(D) The unique class of Yi-hsing wares originated early in the sixteenth century. The best specimens are glossy but unglazed tea pots, which by their shapes and surface treatment are remote from their current fashions. The "pear skin" effect of this particular vessel is due to an admixture of particles of quartz to the reddish brown clay.

A.

C.

D.

B.

PLATE LVII

A. SCHOLAR, Glassy White Porcelain

Late Ming or early Ch'ing dynasty
(17th Century A.D.)
H: 16½"   B60P20+
Published: Garner, *op. cit.*, p. 133, fig. 12

B. KUAN YIN, Glassy White Porcelain

Late Ming or early Ch'ing dynasty
(17th Century A.D.)
H: 7⅜"   B60P36+

The white wares of Te-hua, commonly known in the West as Blancs de Chine,
deserve a special mention. The prosperity of this Fukienese locality can be traced back
to the seventeenth century when it specialized in the manufacture of religious
figures and objects of the cult. This production was so successful that Te-hua was
regarded as the only serious competitor of Ching-te-chen which had since long become
the ceramic capital of China. The enduring fame of Te-hua is largely due to the
exceptional quality of a local clay which permitted plastic experimentations and took
on, after firing, an ivory tone much appreciated by Chinese and Western collectors.

Because of the absence of clear external evidences and of the conservatism in
iconography and technique, late Ming statuettes cannot be told easily from early Ch'ing
figures. Tranquil yet fluid pictures and heavy garments with deep rounded folds
and crisp edges are generally considered to denote a seventeenth century if not late
Ming origin.

A.

B.

PLATE LVIII

A. BOWL, Porcelain, Bisque Dragons on White Ground

Mark and period of Hung Chih
(1488–1505 A.D.)
H: 3½″ D: 7⅞″   B60P2079

B. PLATE, Porcelain, Green Dragons on White Ground

Mark and period of Cheng Te
(1506–1521 A.D.)
H: 1¾″ D: 9″   B60P2091

Starting fom the last decades of the fifteenth century, some imperial kilns revived the kind of polychrome decoration which had been in such great favor during the middle part of the T'ang dynasty (Pls. XIX, and XXV through XXVI). T'ang three-colored pottery was relying exclusively on glazes of different colors, but Ming porcelain of this type also made use of a variety of enamels with a predominance of yellow and green. Conversely, Ming decorative motifs were largely restricted to dragons in incised lines and to bichromatic effects.

The four following items (See also the next plate) illustrate three Ming reigns which paid particular attention to this group, namely those of Hung Chih, Cheng Te, and Chia Ching.

(A) In this particularly subtle effort to achieve subdued bichromatism, the "sunken" dragon was left in reserve on the biscuit. It is slightly off-white whereas the bowl itself is almost pure white.

(B) In ceramic art the origin of the "descending dragon" with its body and tail forming an almost complete circle over its head, goes back to at least the fourteenth century. Yet this peculiar motif was not popularized before the reigns of Hung Chih and Cheng Te when the animal was usually represented in a simple setting of formal clouds.

Here the ornament is painted in green enamel. The body of the dragon and the clouds are underglazed but claws and flames having no incised basis are penciled directly over the glaze.

B.

A.

PLATE LIX

A. JAR, Porcelain, Yellow Designs on Coral-Red Ground

Mark and period of Chia Ching
(1522–1566 A.D.)
H: 5½″ D: 5″   B60P1523

B. BOWL, Porcelain, Green Dragons on Iron-Red Ground

Mark and period of Chia Ching
(1522–1566 A.D.)
H: 2¾″ D: 6⅛″   B60P2081

During the reign of Chia Ching the range of bichromatic effects was enlarged by a number of new colors for motifs and backgrounds. This practice coincided with a taste for more pungent and warmer contrasts.

(A) The ebullient pattern of formal clouds, dragons, waves, and rocks appear in yellow on a coral-red background.

(B) Here an abbreviated version of similar motifs stands in green against a tomato-red background.

B.   *A.*

PLATE LX

A. WINE JAR, Stoneware, Three-Colored Glazes

Fa-hua type
Ming dynasty
(*ca.* 1500 A.D.)
H: 18″ D: 14″   B60P1226
Published: Garner, *op. cit.,* p. 132, fig. 8

B. VASE, Stoneware, Three-Colored Glazes

Fa-hua type
Ming dynasty
(*ca.* 1500 A.D.)
H: 10″ D: 5¼″   B60P1608

The technique known as "fa-hua" or "cloisonné" is another offshoot of the T'ang
three-colored series. It comprises a large group of stoneware jars, vases, and flower pots,
made perhaps as early as the later part of the fifteenth century and as late as the
middle of the sixteenth century. The bulk of the materials, however, is generally
ascribed on stylistic grounds to the turn of the sixteenth century.

This ware is heavily potted, and the decoration, essentially plastic, consists of
multi-colored floral motifs or scenes frequently set up against an openwork background.
To prevent the various glazes from intermingling, color units are surrounded by clay
threads in relief. Favored are white, dark blue, aubergine, and turquoise.

(*A*) Among Taoist subjects one of the most frequent is this scene showing the
Eight Immortals paying court to Shou Lao, the God of Longevity, easily recognizable
by his immense forehead, his benign expression, his deer, and other symbols of
long life (such as the flying crane and the crawling tortoise) which surround him.

A.

B.

PLATE LXI

FISH JAR, Porcelain, Five-Colored Glazes and Enamels

Wu-ts'ai type
Chia Ching mark and period
(1522–1566 A.D.)
H: 17″ D: 17″   B60P78+
Published: Garner *op. cit.,* p. 130, Pl. XIV

Early in the Ming dynasty blue-and-white ware was sometimes enhanced by green
and red overglaze enamels. In the sixteenth century, especially during the reign of Chia
Ching, Lung Ch'ing, and Wan Li, this popular type of decoration became extremely
elaborate. The original colors were extended to five or more, and the ware came
to be known as "wu-ts'ai" or "five color" regardless of the number and tonality of the
enamels utilized. As those manufactured for three-colored glazes, these "wu-ts'ai"
enamels were derived from lead glass tinted with metallic oxides. Bodies were heavily
if not coarsely potted; the craftsmen specializing in this type of ware evidently
aimed at creating surface effects as brilliant and striking as possible. (See also next
plate.)

The Chia-ching period is noted for these large potiches decorated as should be
expected (Pl. LIII) with a variety of Taoist emblems forming a setting for large fishes—
symbols of wealth on account of the similarity in the pronunciation of the Chinese
words for "fish" and "abundance."

PLATE LXII

A. JAR, Porcelain, Five-Colored Glazes and Enamels

Ko-akae type
Early Ming dynasty
(15th Century A.D.)
H: 11½" D: 12½"   B60P507

B. HEXAGONAL VASE, Porcelain, Five-Colored Glazes and Enamels

Mark and period of Lung Ch'ing
(1567–1572 A.D.)
Wu-ts'ai type
H: 10½" D: 7½"   B60P2349
Published: Asia Foundation, *op. cit.*, p. 16, Pl. XII

C. VASE, Porcelain, Five-Colored Glazes and Enamels

Wan Li mark and period
(1573–1615 A.D.)
Wu-ts'ai type
H: 17" D: 9"   B60P56
Published: S. Jenyns, *Ming Pottery and Porcelain*, Pl. 100A

(*A*) This provincial, early specimen is highly regarded by the Japanese connoisseurs as a remarkable example of "ko-akae." Such wares have found their way to Japan and have largely inspired certain classes of Early Edo polychrome wares.

(*B*) During the reign of Lung Ch'ing new shapes and decorative motifs were produced, some of which are, euphemistically, of a "meretricious" order. One of the most refined types is this hexagonal vase with a decoration of antithetical phoenixes.

(*C*) Underglaze blue combined with overglaze enamels reached such a degree of perfection and popularity that Chinese historians usually grant them a special chapter under the title *"Wan Li wu ts'ai."* Together with our Chia Ching potiche (See preceding plate) specialists consider this bottle as a superior example.

A.

B.

C.

PLATE LXIII

A. PLATTER, Porcelain

Polychrome ware
Late Ming dynasty
(17th Century A.D.)
Swatow type
D: 15″   B60P1123

B. PLATTER, Porcelain

Polychrome ware
Late Ming dynasty
(16th to 17th Century A.D.)
Swatow type (probably from Shih-ma)
D: 14″   B60P257

C. PLATTER, Porcelain

Polychrome ware
Late Ming dynasty
(17th Century A.D.)
Swatow type
D: 15″   B60P1124

D. PLATTER, Blue and White Porcelain

Late Ming dynasty
(16th to 17th Century A.D.)
Swatow type (probably from Shih-ma)
D: 14⅝″   B65P43

E. PLATTER, White Decor on Blue Ground

Late Ming dynasty
(17th Century A.D.)
Swatow type
D: 15⁷⁄₁₆″   B65P42

The so-called "Swatow" wares form one of the most important groups of Late Ming provincial ceramics. The main centers of production were probably in Fukien and a large part of their output was exported all over Asia as far as Persia and Japan.

Blue and white dishes, plates, and jars are the most common (D). In many cases the paint was applied directly without preliminary outlines; this, and the use of a versatile wet brush, contributes to create a feeling of improvisation.

Another group (A, B, C) shows red, green, and turquoise enamels, which produce lively, if somewhat naive, effects; yet another group is decorated in white against a blue, green, or brown background (E). In all series ornamental schemes can be typically Chinese or adapted to foreign tastes but they display a verve and an ingenuity not found in more formal categories.

A.

B.

C.

D.

E.

PLATE LXIV

A. VASE, Porcelain

Lang Yao (Sang de boeuf) Glaze
Period of K'ang Hsi
(1662–1722 A.D.)
H: 7¼"   B60P1329

B. MEI-P'ING VASE, Porcelain, Cherry Red Glaze

Period of K'ang Hsi
(1662–1722 A.D.)
H: 9¾"   B60P18

C. VASE, Porcelain, Slip Decoration, Clair de lune Glaze

Period of K'ang Hsi
(1662–1722 A.D.)
H: 7¾"   B60P1273

D. BRUSH WASHER, Porcelain, Slip Decoration, Clair de lune Glaze

K'ang Hsi mark and period
(1662–1722 A.D.)
H: 3" D: 3⅛"   B60P1269

K'ang Hsi monochromes have simple, almost abbreviated shapes and flowing contours.

Many glazes of this period are known in the West under their French names because of the early and detailed records of French residents in China and of the suggestive power of their terminology: Sang de Boef (ox blood, Pl. LXIV-*A* and *A* on this plate), Claire de Lune (moonlight, *C* and *D* on this plate), Cafe au Lait (coffee and milk), Sang de Pigeon (chicken blood), and so on.

French names are also used for some polychrome wares (See next plates for such denominations as Famille Noire (black series), Famille Verte (green series), Mille Fleurs (thousand flower series), and so on.

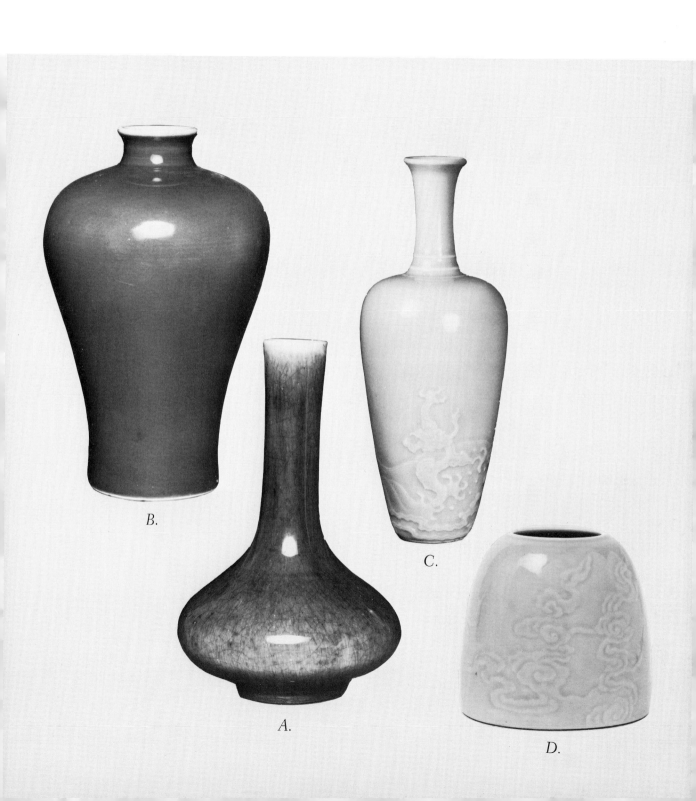

B.

A.

C.

D.

PLATE LXV

A. KU-SHAPED VASE, Porcelain

Lang-yao (Sang de boeuf) Glaze
Period of K'ang Hsi
(1662–1722 A.D.)
H: 7"   B60P1268

B. VASE, Porcelain, Apple-Green Glaze

Period of K'ang Hsi
(1662–1722 A.D.)
H: 6¼"   B60P1312

C. BRUSH WASHER, Porcelain, Peach-Bloom Glaze

Mark and period of K'ang Hsi
(1662–1722 A.D.)
H: 3½" D: 5"   B60P1266

Monochromes of the K'ang Hsi period are characterized by the relative sturdiness of their bodies and the variety and warmth of their thick glazes. Under the guidance of Ts'ang Ying-hsüan, director of the imperial factory at Ching-te chen, unprecedented colors or color effects were introduced with great success as potters improved on the old technique which consisted of tinting feldspathic glazes with metallic oxides.

(A) A number of vessels reflect archaeological interest by imitating ancient bronze shapes, but these are not as laboriously done as the imitations of later period (See for instance Pl. LXXI). The red—very brilliant and even—stops short of the lip and foot rim, and the glaze is finely crackled. A wide range of reds were derived from copper oxide and required very high firing.

(B) Green glazes are technically so close to Lang Yao glazes that they are sometimes mentioned as "Green Lang Yao" and may have been discovered by accident as a result of misfiring. They were produced in various tones.

(C) Peach-bloom glazes can be regarded as standing midway between Lang Yao and "Green Lang Yao." They are usually found in association with small objects for the writer's desk. Often water bottles are decorated with dragon medallions incised under the glaze.

A.

B.

C.

PLATE LXVI

VASE, Porcelain, Enameled Ware

Famille Noire type
Mark and period of K'ang Hsi
(1662–1722 A.D.)
H: 27"   B60P80

This large vase and the next one illustrate the two types of enameled wares for which
the K'ang Hsi period is best known. (See also Pls. LXVII, LXVIII.) Both groups
continue a centuries-old tradition transmitted by Late Ming enamels (Pls. LI through
LIII) but a number of technical and stylistic innovations revolutionized this branch
of Chinese ceramics.

The enamels of the Famille Noire and related groups are applied on the biscuit
in a manner recalling the method used in connection with the Ming three-color wares
(Pls. LVIII, LIX). The iridescence of the background was obtained by covering
black pigment with transparent green enamel. Overall, homogeneous decoration,
different from the usual division in panels or registers, is a characteristic of the ware.
Favorite subjects are adaptations of the category known in Chinese painting as
"Hua-niao" ("Flowers and Birds").

PLATE LXVII

A. BOWL, Porcelain, Enameled Ware

Famille Verte type
Mark and period of K'ang Hsi
(1662–1722 A.D.)
H: 2″ D: 4¾″   B60P183

B. and C. TWO OF A SET OF 12 BOWLS, Porcelain, Underglaze Blue

Enamels of the Famille Verte type
Period of K'ang Hsi
(1662–1722 A.D.)
H: 2″ D: 2½″   B60P1279 and 1291

These three bowls are examples of the most sophisticated series of enameled polychrome porcelain of the late seventeenth or early eighteenth century. They were imitated during all subsequent periods (Pls. LXXIII, LXXIV), but remained unsurpassed and mark a technical climax in the history of ceramic art regardless of age and origin. They were the reward of 2,500 years of sustained effort to create the faultless ware. Bodies are practically of eggshell consistence, the brush work is impeccable, and colors are rich and limpid.

Unfortunately, once accepted as an exclusive standard of excellence, such virtuosity blocked the way to individual research and expression.

Except for a few technical innovations and the ever-increasing influence of Western taste and ideas, the ceramic history of the last 250 years could be described as a nostalgic return to the past.

In 1964 the Chinese government published a lavishly illustrated book on the contemporary production of Ching-te chen. All specimens shown in it are inspired by models dating from the Sung to the Ch'ing dynasties. It would seem that ceramics have remained unaffected by the changes that the revolution brought about in painting, sculpture or some branches of the decorative arts.

(B) and (C) are parts of a set of twelve cups, each unit representing a month of the year. The months illustrated here are those of January (B) and July (C).

A.

B.

C.

PLATE LXVIII

MALLET-SHAPED VASE, Porcelain, Enameled Ware

Famille Verte type
Period of K'ang Hsi
(1662–1722 A.D.)
H: 30″ D: 9″   B60P1237

The Famille Verte, a technical triumph, is an outgrowth of the Ming Wu-ts'ai (Pls. LXI, LXII). With the introduction of a cobalt-blue enamel which can be painted over the glaze like all other enamels in this group, the decorator's palette reaches its full maturity.

Anatomical divisions of vessels are usually observed but there is a new profusion of ornamental schemes. Central motifs frequently represent genre scenes or landscapes. They tend to expand over and around the body in a circular pattern.

Here the main panel depicts an audience at the camp of a Manchu commander-in-chief. On the neck Shou Lao (the God of Longevity, see also Pl. LX) meets T'ien Kuan (the Heavenly Ruler of the Taoist Trinity) whose main function is to bestow happiness. On the shoulder, the four emblems of scholarly accomplishment (the pairs of books and scrolls, lute, and chessboard) alternate with blossoms.

PLATE LXIX

VASE, Porcelain, Enameled Ware

Famille Verte type
Period of K'ang Hsi
(1662–1722 A.D.)
H: 12¼"   B60P2+
Published: Garner, *op. cit.,* p. 132, fig. 9

As potters produced decorative pieces in increasing quantities it became a practice to make for them elaborate stands usually in some other material such as wood or ivory. Some of these stands are *objets d'art* in their own right even though they do not conform with the taste for inconspicuous settings now prevailing in museums.

In this rare specimen the ceramic stand was fired with the vase into an indivisible whole. The wavy pattern was made in imitation of veined wood and recalls that of the "marbled" ware of the T'ang and Sung periods. (Pl. XXXVII).

To appreciate the stylistic and technical changes that took place during the seven hundred years since painting on glazed ceramics was making its beginnings, compare this vase with the pillow C of Plate XL.

PLATE LXX

A. VASE, Porcelain

Glaze of Kuan type
Mark and period of Yung Cheng
(1723–1735 A.D.)
H: 9½″   B60P2280

B. EWER, Porcelain

Celadon Glaze
Mark and period of Yung Cheng
(1723–1735 A.D.)
H: 10″   B60P13

C. MEI-P'ING VASE, Porcelain, Tea-Dust Glaze

Mark and period of Yung Cheng
(1723–1735 A.D.)
H: 10″   B60P16

During the comparatively short reign of Yung Cheng the production of monochromes was marked by three main tendencies: revival of some Sung series, imitations of ancient bronze vessels, and introduction of new glaze effects. Nien Hsi-yao, whose career as director of the imperial factory spans the Yung Cheng period, is given credit for all these styles.

(A) Yung Cheng "Kuan Yao" are among the most successful recaptures of the classical wares of the Sung period (Pl. XLV). At times the similarity is striking, yet, in most cases, Yung Cheng bodies are purer, crisper, and with edges much sharper than those of their models. Yung Cheng glazes are also extremely dense by comparison with Sung glazes, whose bubbles can almost be seen with the naked eye.

(B) It would be difficult to find a better illustration of the syncretic tendencies prevailing during this period. By its shape and decorative motifs, this handleless ewer is an adaptation of a contemporary blue-and-white ware decorated in the Hsüan Te styles (Pl. LXXII). Its glaze exemplifies one of the numerous celadon tones which were made in imitation of Sung prototypes (Pl. XLIV).

(C) Tea dust is one of the glaze effects introduced during the directorship of Nien Hsi-Yao. It results from the insufflation of green enamel upon an iron-brown ground.

A.

B.

C.

PLATE LXXI

KU-SHAPED VASE, Porcelain, Creamy White Glaze

    Soft paste type
    Yung Cheng mark and period
    (1723–1735 A.D.)
    H: 7⅜"   B60P1789

Soft paste (or "paste-bodied porcelain" as the Chinese would say) is a K'ang Hsi innovation and ranked among the most expensive ware because it called for the use of special ingredients and was difficult to control. It is characterized by its thinness, lightness, and fragility. It has an undulating surface with very fine crazing.

    This Ku shows the archaistic molded pattern characteristic of the period. This is less an imitation of an ancient bronze vessel than a plastic rendering of the line-drawings published in many archaeological treatises of the Sung, Ming, and Ch'ing dynasties.

PLATE LXXII

A. EWER, Blue and White Porcelain

Period of Yung Cheng
(1723–1735 A.D.)
H: 14"   B60P85

B. PILGRIM BOTTLE, Blue and White Porcelain

Mark and period of Ch'ien Lung
(1736–1795 A.D.)
H: 19" D: 14"   B60P89

C. MEI-P'ING VASE, Porcelain, Underglaze Red Decoration

Hsüan Te mark, period of Ch'ien Lung
(1736–1795 A.D.)
H: 13½"   B60P81

During the reigns of Yung Cheng and Ch'ien Lung the fifteenth-century blue-and-white was revived. The blue was "piled up" and darkened to give the illusion of the impure cobalt used by early Ming potters. Recaptures, frequently antedated, ranged from copies (A) to more or less imaginative transposition (B and C), but even in the closest parallels, the color was spotted in an artificial and mechanical way, which leaves no doubt about their late origin.

(A) The eighteenth-century potter wanted to imitate not only the technique but also the mood of his early fifteenth-century predecessors, thus baffling the casual observer. Such nearly perfect imitations are fairly rare. (See for comparison Pl. LII.)

(B) Both shapes and ornamental schemes are inspired by much earlier types but the potter has introduced some extra features such as the spiraling handles and the splaying foot. Also, his central rosette has the stiffness characteristic of the Ch'ien Lung period when geometrical patterns were the rule.

(C) Despite its Hsüan Te mark, this vase retains only one feature of its fifteenth century prototypes, namely the row of "false gadroons" on the shoulder. The bulging shoulder, the disconnected branches of the central zone, and the "realistic" leaves on the foot, all point to an eighteenth-century date.

B.

C.

A.

PLATE LXXIII

A. PLATE, Porcelain

Enamels of the Famille Rose type
Yung Cheng mark and period
(1723–1735 A.D.)
D: 5¼″   B60P1697

B. BOWL, Porcelain

Famille Rose enamels on Coral red ground
Yung Cheng mark and period
(1723–1735 A.D.)
D: 5¾″   B60P2086

C. BOWL AND COVER, Porcelain

Tou-ts'ai type
Yung Cheng mark and period
(1723–1735 A.D.)
H: 6″ D: 8″   B60P2108
Published: Jenyns, *Later Chinese Porcelain*
Pl. XCIV, fig. 3

(*A*) and (*B*) During the administration of Nien Hsi-yao the transparent colors of the Famille Verte were superseded by a set of opaque enamels which had been experimentally used during the last years of the K'ang Hsi period. This new set is known in the West as Famille Rose and in China as "foreign color." Both terms reflect the introduction of a rose pink discovered in Europe in the middle of the seventeenth century, resulting from a combination of gold chloride and tin. Together with a number of shapes and ornamental schemes, this innovation is one of the major Western contributions to the development of Chinese porcelains during the later part of the Ch'ing dynasty.

(*C*) In spite of the rapidly increasing popularity of the Famille Rose, some early Yung Cheng potters revived the old "tou ts'ai" ("conflicting colors") technique as it had been practised during the Ming dynasty since the reign of Ch'eng Hua. Although the painter's palette is considerably richer and more brilliant, the revival is conscious. Underglaze blue outlines are often emphasized, and ornamental schemes borrow from the Ming stock of motifs.

C.

A.

B.

PLATE LXXIV

A. VASE, Porcelain, Enameled Ware

Famille Rose type
Mark and period of Ch'ien Lung
(1736–1795 A.D.)
H: 12¼″   B60P65
Published: Jenyns, *op. cit.*, Pl. CIX, No. 2

B. BOWL, Porcelain, Enameled Ware

Mille Fleurs type
Mark and period of Chia Ch'ing
(1796–1821 A.D.)
H: 2⅝″ D: 5⅛″   B60P2095

C. BOWL, Porcelain, Gray and Black Enameled on Yellow Ground

Period of Kuang Hsü
(1875–1908 A.D.)
H: 3⅜″ D: 7″   B60P1558

The first part of the reign of Ch'ien Lung was marked by the administration of T'ang
Ying, the last of the great directors of the imperial factory. Thereafter begins
the period of decline, characterized by technicality which, however, does not always
succeed in stifling completely the inventiveness and superb craftsmanship which
have always been the outstanding qualities of the Chinese potter.

(A) During the later part of the eighteenth-century polychrome series were mostly
decorated with enamels of the Famille Rose type. Here they have been engraved
in "graviata" designs. Two sides of the vase show paneled landscapes in Four Wang
style.

(B) Here also each element of this crowded pattern is circumscribed by engraved
lines.

(C) This bowl was part of a set made for the Empress Dowager Tz'u Hsi who ruled
China during the last decades of the nineteenth century and the first years of the
twentieth century. Among other inscriptions it bears near the rim the hall-mark of one
of the residences of the Empress, the Ta Ya Chai (Studio of Great Refinement).

A.

C.

B.

PLATE LXXV

VASE, Porcelain, Enameled Ware

Famille Rose type
Mark and period of Ch'ien Lung
(1736–1795 A.D.)
H: 19"   B60P124+

During the Ch'ing dynasty symbols of longevity, wealth, and happiness remained favorite motifs. The peach symbolized immortality when associated with Shou Lao (Pls. LX, LXIX); it was also an emblem of marriage and a symbol of spring.

The mark of this monumental vase is written in seal characters. The habit of using this most formal and also most stilted style of Chinese calligraphy to mark porcelain became common in the eighteenth century (Pl. LIII).

Chronology

NEOLITHIC	*ca.* 2500–1500 B.C.
SHANG	*ca.* 1523–1028 B.C.
CHOU	*ca.* 1027– 222 B.C.
Western Chou	*ca.* 1027–771 B.C.
Ch'un-ch'iu	770–481 B.C.
Warring States	480–222 B.C.
CH'IN	221–207 B.C.
HAN	206 B.C.–A.D. 220
Western Han	206 B.C.–A.D. 8
Eastern Han	A.D. 25–220
THE THREE KINGDOMS	221–265
THE SIX DYNASTIES	265–589
SUI	589–618
T'ANG	618–906
THE FIVE DYNASTIES	906–960
SUNG	960–1279
Northern Sung	960–1127
Southern Sung	1127–1279
Liao	907–1125
Chin	1115–1234
YÜAN	1280–1368
MING	1368–1644

Hung Wu	1368–1398	Chia Ching	1522–1566
Yung Lo	1403–1424	Lung Ch'ing	1567–1572
Hsüan Te	1426–1435	Wan Li	1573–1619
Ch'eng Hua	1465–1467	T'ien Ch'i	1621–1627
Cheng Te	1506–1521	Ch'ung Chen	1628–1644

CH'ING 1644–1912

K'ang Hsi	1662–1722	Chia Ch'ing	1796–1820
Yung Cheng	1723–1735	Tao Kuang	1821–1850
Ch'ien Lung	1736–1795	Kuang Hsü	1875–1908

Selected Bibliography

BOOKS AND ARTICLES

Ch'en Wan-li   *Sung-tai Pei-fang Min-chien Tz'u-ch'i,* (Northern-type Folk Porcelains of the Sung Period), Peking 1955

Chung-kuo Ch'ing-tz'u Shih Lüeh, (Brief History of Chinese Celadon Wares), Shanghai 1956

T'ao Yung, (Clay Figurines), Peking 1957

Cheng Te-k'un   *Archaeology in China,* 3 volumes, Cambridge 1959–1963

Chiang Hsüan-t'ai   *Chi-chou Yao,* (Chi-chou Kilns), Peking 1958

Ching-te chên T'ao-tz'u I-shu (Ceramic Art at Ching-te Chên), Peking 1964

Cox, Warren   *The Book of Pottery and Porcelain,* New York 1944

Fu Chen-lun   *Ming-tai Tz'u-ch'i Kung-i* (Ming Porcelains), Peking 1955

Fu Yang   *Ming-tai Min-chien Ch'ing-hua Tz'ü-ch'i* (Folk Blue and White Porcelains of the Ming Period), Peking 1957

Garner, Harry   *Oriental Blue and White,* London 1954

"Sung and Later Ceramic Wares in The Avery Brundage Collection," *Apollo,* August 1966, pp. 126–133

Goidsenhaven, J. P. van   *La Céramique Chinoise,* Bruxelles 1954

Gompertz, G. St. G. M.   *Chinese Celadon Wares,* London 1958

Gray, Basil   *Early Chinese Pottery and Porcelain,* London 1953

Hobson, R. L. and Hetherington, A. L.   *The Art of the Chinese Potter, from The Han Dynasty to the End of the Ming,* London 1923

Hochstadter, Walter   "Pottery and Stonewares of Shang, Chou and Han" in *Bulletin of the Museum of Far Eastern Antiquities,* Stockholm, 1952, No. 24, pp. 81 and ff

Honey, William B.   *The Ceramic Art of China and Other Countries in the Far East,* London 1945

Hsü P'ing-yü   *Nan-ching Fu-chin K'ao-ku Pao-kao* (Report on Archaeological Work in the Vicinity of Nanking), Shanghai 1952

Hunan Province Cultural Committee   *Ch'ang-sha Fa-chüeh Pao-kao* (Report on Excavations at Ch'ang-sha), Ch'ang-sha 1957

Jenyns, Soames	*Later Chinese Porcelain,* London 1951
	Ming Pottery and Porcelain, London 1953
Kiangsu Province Cultural Committee	*Nan-ching Ch'u-t'u Liu-ch'ao Ch'ing-tz'u* (Six Dynasties Celadons Excavated at Nanking), Peking 1957
Koyama, Fujio	*Shina Seiji Shikō* (Notes on the History of Chinese Celadon), Tokyo 1943
	Sekai Tōji Zenshū (Catalogue of the World's Ceramics), Vols. 8–12, Tokyo 1954–1957
	Céramique Ancienne de L'Asie, Fribourg 1959
Lefebvre d' Argencé, R.-Y.	"Early Chinese Ceramics in The Avery Brundage Collection." *Apollo,* August 1966, pp. 84–102
Lefebvre d'Argencé, R.-Y., Cahill, James and Yashiro Yukio	"The Avery Brundage Collection of Asian Art" in *Asia Foundation Program Bulletin,* Special Issue, San Francisco, August 1966
Liao-ning Provincial Museum	*Liao Tz'u Hsüan-chi* (Selected Items of Liao Pottery), Peking 1961
Lion-Goldschmidt, D. and Moreau, Gobard J.C.	*Les Poteries et Porcelaines Chinoises,* Paris 1957
Mahler, J. C.	*The Westerners Among the Figurines of the T'ang Dynasty of China,* Rome 1959
Mizuno, S. and others	*Sekai Kōkogaku Taikei,* Vols. 5, 6, 7, Tokyo 1958
Paine, R. T.	"Chinese Ceramic Pillows" in *Far Eastern Ceramic Bulletin,* Vol. VII, No. 3 (Serial No. 31) September 1955
Pope, J. A.	*Chinese Porcelains from the Ardebil Shrine,* Washington 1956
Prodan, M.	*The Art of the T'ang Potter,* New York 1960
Sekai Bijutsu Taikei	*Chugoku Bijutsu* (Arts of the World series: Chinese Art), Edited Kodansha, Tokyo 1963
Shen Chung-ch'ang and others	*Ssu-ch'uan Han-tai T'ao-yung* (Szechwanese Clay Figurines of the Han Period), Peking 1963
Shensi Provincial Museum	*Yao-tz'u T'u-lu* (Illustrated Catalogue of Yao Wares), Peking 1956
Shensi Province Cultural Committee	*Shensi T'ang San-ts'ai Yung* (Three-color Figurines of the T'ang Dynasty Found in Shensi Province), Peking 1964
Shensi Provincial Research Institute	*Shensi T'ung-ch'uan Yao-chou Yao* (The Kao-chou Kilns, Near T'ung-ch'uan in Shensi Province), Peking 1965

Tanaka, S. and others	*Chugoku no Tōji* (Chinese Ceramics), Tokyo 1955
	Tōki Zenshu (Complete Collection of Ceramics) published by Heibonsha, Vols. 9–16 and 25–27
Umehara, S.	*Kanan Anyō Ibutsu no Kenkyū* (Research on Relics from An-yang, Honan), Kyoto 1941
Umezawa, H. and others	*Min-Dai no Sometsuke to Akae* (Ming Blue and White and Enameled Porcelain), Tokyo 1952
Wu, G. D.	*Prehistoric Pottery in China*, London 1938

PERIODICALS

Archives of the Chinese Art Society of America

Bulletin of the Museum of Far Eastern Antiquities, Stockholm, No. 15, 17, 24

Far Eastern Ceramic Bulletin, Boston, Massachusetts

Kaogu, 1959, Nos. 1, 11; 1960 No. 9, Peking

Kaogu Xuebao, 1955; 1956, No. 3; 1957; No. 1; 1958, Nos. 1 & 2 Peking

Oriental Art, London

Transactions of the Oriental Ceramic Society, London, Vols. 14, 18, 21, 26, 29, 30, and 31

Wen Wu (Ts'an-k'ao Ts'ai-liao), 1954 No. 10; 1960 No. 11; 1964 Nos. 8 and 12; 1965 Nos. 6, 10; 1966 No. 3, Peking

CATALOGUES OF COLLECTIONS AND EXHIBITIONS

Ayers, John	*The Seligman Collection of Oriental Art*, Vol. II: *Chinese and Korean Pottery and Porcelain*, London 1964
Ch'en Wan-li	*Ku-kung Po-wu-yüan Ts'ang Tz'u Hsüan-chi* (Selected Porcelains from the Collections of the Palace Museum) Wu Press, Peking 1962
Dubosc, J. P.	*Exhibition of Chinese Art*, Venice 1954
Hobson, R. L.	*Catalogue of the George Eumorfopoulos Collection of Chinese*, etc. *Pottery and Porcelain*, 6 vols. London 1925–1928
La Plante, John D.	*Arts of the Chou dynasty*, Stanford University Museum 1958
Loehr, Max	*Relics of Ancient China from the Collection of Dr. Paul Singer*, Asia House 1965, New York

Loo, C. T.   *Exhibition of Chinese Art,* New York 1941–42.

Mayuyama, J.   *Chinese Ceramics in the West,* Tokyo 1960

Royal Academy of Arts   *Catalogue of the International Exhibition of Chinese Art,* London 1935–1936

Sullivan, Michael   *Chinese Ceramics Bronzes and Jades in the Barlow Collection,* London 1963

Tomita, K.   *The Charles B. Hoyt Collection,* Boston 1952

Tokyo National Museum   *Illustrated Catalogue of Old Oriental Ceramics donated by Mr. Yokogawa,* Tokyo 1953

Trubner, Henry   *Chinese Ceramics,* Los Angeles County Museum 1952

                              The Arts of the T'ang Dynasty, Los Angeles County Museum 1957